THE ROUGH GUIDE TO
Trumpet &
Trombone
Flugelhorn & Cornet

Whether you're a beginner or a pro,
whether you are about to buy an instrument
or you want to learn more about the one
you already have – this book is for you.

Hugo Pinksterboer

THE ES

Publishing Details

This first edition published May 2001 by Rough Guides Ltd,
62–70 Shorts Gardens, London WC2H 9AH

Distributed by the Penguin Group:
Penguin Books Ltd, 27 Wrights Lane, London W8 5TZ
Penguin Putnam, Inc., 375 Hudson Street, New York, NY 10014
Penguin Books Australia Ltd, 487 Maroondah Highway, PO Box
257, Ringwood, Victoria 3134, Australia
Penguin Books Canada Ltd, 10 Alcorn Avenue, Toronto, Ontario,
Canada M4V 1E4
Penguin Books (NZ) Ltd, 182–190 Wairau Road, Auckland 10,
New Zealand

Typeset in Glasgow and Minion to an original design by
The Tipbook Company bv

Printed in The Netherlands by Hentenaar Boek bv, Nieuwegein

© The Tipbook Company bv, 2000

144 pp

A catalogue record for this book is available from the British
Library.
1-85828-754-5

3

THE ROUGH GUIDE TO

Trumpet & Trombone

Flugelhorn & Cornet

Written by

Hugo Pinksterboer

ROUGH GUIDES

THE ESSENTIAL TIPBOOK

Rough Guide Tipbook Credits

Journalist, writer and musician **Hugo Pinksterboer** has written hundreds of articles and reviews for international music magazines. He is the author of the reference work for cymbals (*The Cymbal Book*, Hal Leonard, US) and has written and developed a wide variety of musical manuals and courses.

Illustrator, designer and musician **Gijs Bierenbroodspot** has worked as an art director in advertising and for magazines. While searching in vain for information about saxophone mouthpieces, he came up with the idea for this series of books on music and musical instruments. Since then, he has created the layout and the illustrations for all of the books.

Acknowledgements

Concept, design and illustrations: Gijs Bierenbroodspot

Translation: MdJ Copy & Translation

Editor: Duncan Clark

IN BRIEF

Have you just started playing? Are you thinking about buying a trumpet, a trombone, a flugelhorn or a cornet? Or do you just want to know more about the instrument you already own? This book will tell you everything you need to know. You'll read about the names of all the parts and what they do, about lessons and practising and about tuning and maintenance, and there are tips about what you should look and listen for when purchasing an instrument or choosing a mouthpiece or mute. The book also contains a summary of the main manufacturers, a brief history of the instruments, and a section on the other members of the brass instrument family.

Valuable knowledge

After reading this book you will have all the information you need to make a good choice when you go to buy an instrument. What's more, you'll know enough to be able to make sense of magazines, brochures, Web sites and books on the subject.

The first four chapters

If you have only just started playing, or haven't yet begun, pay special attention to the first four chapters. If you've been playing for longer, you may want to skip ahead to Chapter 5.

Glossary

Most of the terms you'll come across in this book are briefly explained in the glossary at the end, which doubles as an index.

CONTENTS

1. BRASS INSTRUMENTS

If you play the trumpet, trombone, flugelhorn or cornet, that makes you a brass player. They are all wind instruments made of brass, and they are all played in roughly the same way.

On a guitar it's the strings that vibrate. On a drum it's the skin. On a brass instrument it's your lips. If you put your lips together and blow through them you can make a sound like air escaping from a balloon, but you can also make a sound like an engine. In the same way, you can make a trumpet or a trombone make lots of very different sounds – from high to low, from crisp to mellow.

Trumpets and trombones

Trumpets and trombones appear in lots of styles of music – from jazz and salsa to orchestral classical music. Some groups may have just one trumpeter and one trombonist, whilst a symphony orchestra can have many of each.

Flugelhorns

The flugelhorn, which sounds fuller, warmer and more mellow than a trumpet, is an important instrument in brass bands. But there's also a good chance of hearing a flugelhorn at a jazz or classical concert, in which case it will usually be played by a trumpeter.

Cornets

The cornet falls somewhere between a flugelhorn and a trumpet: it sounds less mellow than a flugelhorn, yet less brilliant and piercing than a trumpet. The cornet is the main instrument in brass bands, but you may also come across cornets in old-style jazz bands and classical orchestras.

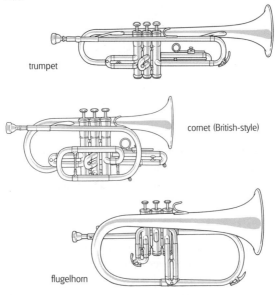

trumpet

cornet (British-style)

flugelhorn

The cornet is somewhere between a flugelhorn and a trumpet

Wind and brass

Wind instruments are any instruments that you blow into, and they are divided into two main categories: *brass instruments*, such as those covered in this book, and *woodwind instruments*, such as clarinets and flutes. Brass instruments are nearly always made of brass, but woodwind instruments are not necessarily made of wood (saxophones and flutes, for example, are made of metal). However, the terms aren't set in stone – the term 'wind instruments' is sometimes used just to refer to woodwind, and *brasswind* can mean either brass instruments or brass and woodwind instruments.

Wind bands

Groups that consist mainly of wind players are referred to as *concert bands*, *wind bands* or *wind orchestras*. Large ensembles consisting only of brass players (and a couple of percussionists) are called *brass bands*. You can read more about such groups in Chapter 14.

Classical music

Brass players are also an essential to many styles of classical music, from the wind quintet to the symphony orchestra. The brass section is usually situated at the back of an orchestra, as its sound carries so well.

Jazz

Brass players will generally have much more to play if they are in some kind of jazz ensemble, whether it be a quintet or a big band, or in a soul or salsa group. As well as ensemble playing, there are also opportunities to play improvised solos. In some other styles, the brass instruments are there mainly to give extra colour to the sound.

The horn

Many brass and saxophone players refer to their instrument as a 'horn'. However, there is also an instrument actually called the horn – the *French horn* – which you can read about on page 104–105.

Three buttons or a slide

After only a few months playing a brass instrument, you'll be able to play quite a lot of songs or melodies, but that doesn't mean it's easy to learn. Brass instruments may look quite simple, with just three 'buttons' or one long slide, but in many ways that makes it harder: you don't have a separate button or key for each note.

A trombone looks very simple

No strings attached

You can buy a good trumpet or trombone without paying a fortune. And unlike some instruments, they don't need replacement, strings, reeds, batteries, drum-heads, sticks or picks. You need little more than your instrument, a mouthpiece, a case and the odd drop of lubricant.

2. A QUICK TOUR

The four instruments dealt with in this book are similar to each other in many ways – especially the trumpet, cornet and flugelhorn. This chapter explains the differences and similarities, and tells you what all the bits of the instruments are called and what they all do.

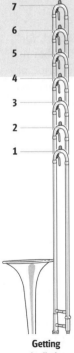

7
6
5
4
3
2
1

**Getting
gradually lower
in seven steps**

Trumpets and trombones are more alike than you might think. A trumpet is a long tube with three *valves*; a trombone is a long tube with an extendable *slide*. You need those valves or the slide to be able to play all the different notes.

A few notes

On a brass instrument without valves or a slide you can only play about seven or eight notes, known as the *harmonics* or *harmonic series*. You can't make much music with just those notes – they're not enough even for most nursery rhymes.

A little longer, a little lower

Using the slide or the valves you can make the tube of the instrument a little longer, and this lowers the pitch of the note. Using valves you can lower the pitch by a *semitone* or *half-step* at a time; with a slide you can lower the pitch continuously. And at each new pitch you can play a whole new harmonic series.

Seven positions, seven series

It's easy to see that a trombone gets longer when you extend the slide. Trombonists play notes at seven different *positions*, from the completely closed *first position* to the fully extended *seventh position*. Moving the slide from one position to the next makes the pitch lower by one semitone. And in each position you can play a whole new harmonic series of notes, which add up to all the notes you could want.

Valves

A trumpet works in basically the same way. The three valves allow you to do the same thing as the slide of a trombone: you keep on making the tube a little longer each time, in seven steps.

Without valves

If you don't press any of the valves, the air passes through the main tube of the instrument only – from the mouthpiece to the valves, and from the valves directly to the bell. You can play a series of some seven or eight notes.

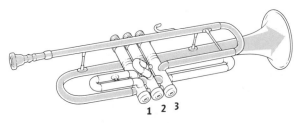

Through the main tube only – the notes you can play without using your valves include low C and the G, C and E above it.

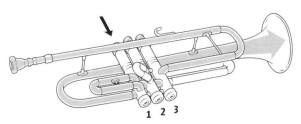

The extra length from the first valve makes the instrument sound a whole tone lower. Now you can play notes like low B flat and the F, B flat and D above it.

Valve 2, one semitone lower

If you press down the second valve, the air also passes through the small U-shaped tube attached to the valve. This makes the tube of the trumpet slightly longer, enabling you to play seven or eight notes that sound a semitone lower.

Valve 1, a whole tone lower

The U-shaped tube of the first valve, closest to the mouthpiece, is about twice as long as the tube of the second valve. If you press just the first valve, you can play a series of notes that sound a *whole tone*, or *whole step*, lower than those produced with no valves.

Valve 3, one and a half tones lower

The tube attached to the third valve is about as long as the combined tubes of the first and second valves. Pressing just the third valve, then, allows for playing a series of notes that sounds one and a half tones lower than the one produced with no valves.

Three valves, seven series

In the same way that a trombone produces seven harmonic series of notes in its seven slide positions, the three valves of a trumpet also allow for seven 'positions', and therefore seven series. This can easily be shown using numbers – 0 means not pressing any valves, 1 means the first valve is pressed down, and so on. The following order is how you lower the sound, semitone by semitone, like the steps of a trombone: 0, 1, 2, 1+2 (or 3 on its own), 2+3, 1+3, 1+2+3 (all the valves pressed down). The three valves on a flugelhorn or a cornet work in exactly the same way.

THE TRUMPET

A trumpet is really a very simple instrument. It's a long tube which has two bends or *bows* in it, and three valves which allow you to play any note you want by varying the length of the tube. But if you take a closer look, there is much more to see.

Mouthpiece

Like all other brass instruments, a trumpet has a detachable mouthpiece that you put against your lips. To make playing

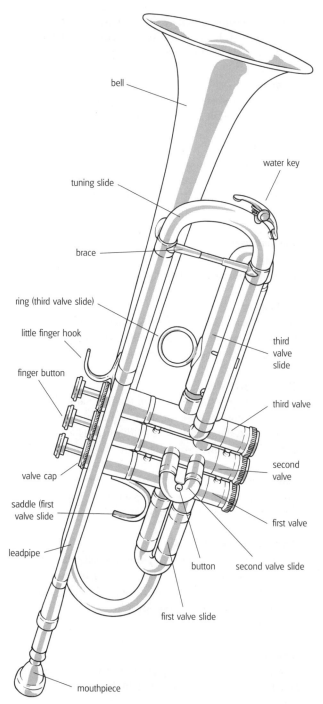

bell

water key

tuning slide

brace

ring (third valve slide)

little finger hook

finger button

third valve slide

third valve

second valve

valve cap

saddle (first valve slide

leadpipe

first valve

button

second valve slide

first valve slide

mouthpiece

as easy as possible, you'll need to find the mouthpiece that suits you best. It must suit the strength of your lips, for example, and even the position of your teeth.

Leadpipe

The mouthpiece sticks into the *mouthpiece receiver*, which is connected to the *leadpipe* or *mouthpipe*.

Tuning slide

The leadpipe ends in the *tuning slide* or *tuning crook*. This is the first bow of the trumpet, starting from the mouthpiece. You tune the trumpet by moving the tuning slide in and out.

The third valve

Past the tuning slide, you come to the third valve. The piece of tubing attached to it is the *third valve slide*.

Fine-tuning

The ring attached to the third valve slide is known as a *throw ring*. It allows you to extend the slide a short distance whilst playing to fine-tune certain notes.

The first valve slide

You can usually fine-tune using the first valve slide too. Some instruments use a ring for that purpose, others have a *first valve slide saddle* or *U-pull*, which is a U-shaped piece of metal which your thumb fits in.

Finger buttons

You operate the valves by pressing down the *finger buttons*, which are often inlaid with real or imitation mother-of-pearl.

Pistons and valve casings

In each *valve casing*, there's a *piston*: a small cylinder with holes in that can direct the air either straight through the valve (if the piston is up), or through the valve slide (if you have moved the piston down by pressing the finger button).

Valve caps

If you unscrew the *valve caps*, you can remove the pistons. You'll need to do so to clean and oil the valves.

The bell

The *bell* is the end of the trumpet which flares outwards, but it also includes the last bend. So the bell actually starts just after the *valve group* or *valve cluster*, which consists of the three valves.

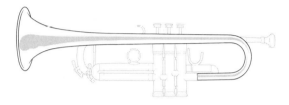

The bell starts right after the valves

Braces

To make a trumpet a little sturdier, it has a *brace* between the bell and the leadpipe, and usually another just before the tuning slide.

Little finger hook

On top of the leadpipe, just after the third valve finger button, there is a hook for the little finger of the right hand.

Water keys

If you stand with your face close to a mirror and breathe on it, the condensation moisture from your breath will 'mist up' the mirror. Much the same thing happens inside your instrument. After you have been playing for a while, so much moisture collects in the instrument that it gives a slightly 'spluttering' sound. This is why a trumpet has *water keys*. Just press the key, blow through the instrument soundlessly and the water is gone.

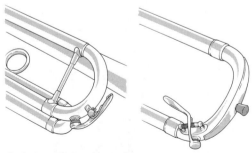

Water key on a trumpet and a trombone

Lyre holder

If you are a marching musician, you can use a *lyre* to attach sheet music to your instrument. Some instruments have a special *lyre holder* to clip it onto, but if your instrument doesn't, you can get a lyre which fixes on with a clamp. Other lyres, as shown in the diagram below, attach to the holder of the third valve slide ring, disabling the use of this slide for fine-tuning.

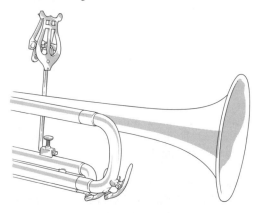

Lyre attached to the holder of the third valve slide ring

THE FLUGELHORN

On a flugelhorn, the bends in the tube are much less sharp than on a trumpet. This makes it look rounder – and it also sounds 'rounder' than a trumpet.

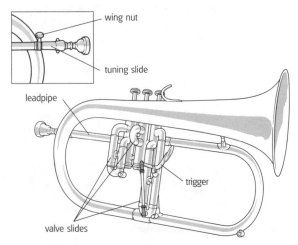

wing nut

tuning slide

leadpipe

trigger

valve slides

A wider flare

The mellow sound of a flugelhorn, compared to a trumpet, is mainly due to the fact that the tube is narrow to begin with and then flares out much wider than on a trumpet. It has a very *conical bore*, to use technical terms. The tube of a flugelhorn becomes rapidly wider from the first bend.

A shorter leadpipe

Another difference is that a flugelhorn's leadpipe is much shorter than a trumpet's. On a flugelhorn, the leadpipe directly connects with the first valve.

Tuning

You tune a flugelhorn by sliding the mouthpiece receiver in and out. When the instrument's in tune, you fix the tube in position with a wing nut.

Vertical valve slides and triggers

Unlike a trumpet, most flugelhorns have vertical first and third valve slides. You can't operate a vertical valve slide with a ring or a hook. That's why most flugelhorns have one or two *triggers*. If you press a trigger lever, it makes the slide a little longer. When you let it go, it automatically returns to its original position.

Fluegelhorn or valved bugle

The flugelhorn or *fluegelhorn*, as it's sometimes spelt, is also referred to as the *valved bugle*.

THE CORNET

There are two basic types of cornet: the *British* or *European*, and the *American*. The most obvious difference is that the British cornet looks much shorter, which explains why it's also known as the *short cornet*, and the American is known as the *long cornet*. But if you were to roll them both out, you'd find that both types are the same length as each other – and the same length as a trumpet or flugelhorn.

In between

The short cornet is a little closer to a flugelhorn than the long cornet, which is more like a trumpet. It's quite easy to hear the difference: the flugelhorn has the fullest, smoothest, most mellow sound, followed by the short cornet, then the long cornet, and finally the trumpet, which has the most bright, piercing sound.

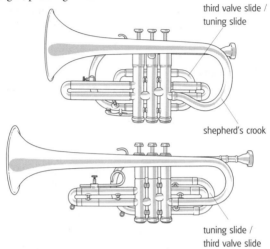

British- and American-style cornets. On both models, the third valve slide sticks out some way beyond the first bend.

Shepherd's crook
The short cornet has a small extra bend, just before the bow of the bell section. This piece of tubing looks a little like the curl of a *shepherd's crook*, and that's what it's called.

The tuning slide
On most cornets, the tube has three bends between the mouthpiece and the third valve. The tuning slide is in the second bend.

Rings and hooks
Just like trumpets, many cornets have a ring on the third valve slide and a hook on the first.

THE TROMBONE
When people talk about trombones they usually mean the *tenor trombone*. This instrument is roughly twice as long as a trumpet. As a result, it sounds one octave lower (eight white keys on a piano makes one octave).

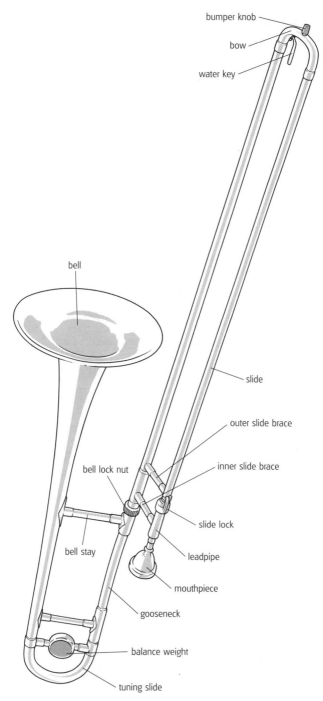

bumper knob

bow

water key

bell

slide

outer slide brace

inner slide brace

bell lock nut

slide lock

bell stay

leadpipe

mouthpiece

gooseneck

balance weight

tuning slide

A big mouthpiece

A trombone tube is around nine feet long (nearly 3m) with the slide closed, and about twelve feet with the slide fully extended. It takes a pretty big mouthpiece to make the air vibrate throughout that whole length.

Two parts

The trombone consists of two main parts: the *bell section* and the *slide*. The two are fixed together with the *bell lock nut*. Trombonists often use the word 'bell' to refer to the entire bell section. The large bow at the back end is the tuning slide.

Inner and outer slides

The slide consists of an *outer slide* which is extended over the tubing of the *inner slide*. You move the outer slide with your right hand, gripping the *outer brace*. Your left hand holds the instrument at the *inner brace*, which is attached to the inner slide.

inner slide

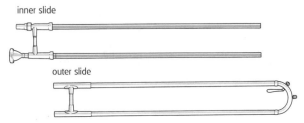

outer slide

Trombone slide

Lock and knob

When you are not playing, the *slide lock* keeps the slide in place. Another security feature is the small rubber *bumper knob* on the bow of the slide, near the water key.

Balance weight

The *bell stay* or *body brace* strengthens the bow of the bell and often has a *balance weight* or *balancer* in its centre. This weight makes it a little easier to hold the instrument without the weight of the slide tipping it forwards.

Trombones with valves

There are also trombones which have either one or two valves. A trombone with two valves is a *bass trombone*.

HOW HIGH AND LOW?

In the case of a brass instrument, there is no simple answer to the question of how high or low it is possible to play. If you're fairly proficient on a trumpet or trombone you'll probably have a range of around two and a half octaves (you can see how much this is on the piano keyboard diagrams below). But there is no set limit to how high it is possible to go, and some people can play three and a half octaves, or even more. When you are just starting out, your range will be much smaller.

Cornets and flugelhorns

Cornets and flugelhorns have basically the same range as trumpets, but most players can go just a little higher on a trumpet.

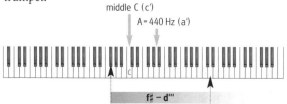

The standard range of a trumpet, cornet or flugelhorn

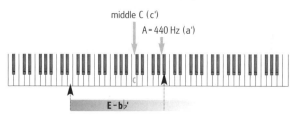

The standard range of a trombone

Octaves and notes

An octave is the musical distance – or *interval* – from one note to the next note of the same name, such as from one C to the next C. In the diagrams above, you'll notice that the note names are written in various different ways – E, a' and d''', and so on. This is a systems of writing down note names that allows you to refer to a specific note at a specific octave. You can read more about this and other systems of naming notes in *The Rough Guide to Reading Music and Basic Theory*. Also marked on the diagram are middle C, which is the C that lies in the middle of the piano keyboard, and the tuning note A = 440 Hz which is explained on page 80.

IN B FLAT

If you're a trumpeter and you see the note C in your music, you will play a 'C' – the note without any valves pressed down. But if you try to find the same note on a piano you will discover that what you're hearing is not a C but a B flat.

Concert pitch

In other words: when a trumpeter plays a C, you hear *concert pitch B flat*. This makes a trumpet a *B flat instrument*, to use the technical term. Most cornets and flugelhorns are B flat instruments too.

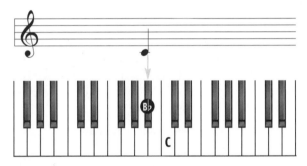

Most trumpets are in B flat: when you read and finger a C, the resulting note sounds the same as a B flat played on a piano.

Transposed

So, composers write a C in a piece of trumpet music when they want to hear a B flat. In the same way every other note is written a whole tone higher than the desired note – they write a D if they want to hear a C, for example, and an F♯ if they want to hear an E. This is called *a transposed part* – and when you play, your trumpet transposes the music back again, so to speak. That's why a trumpet is called a *transposing instrument*. You simply play what your sheet music says, and your trumpet makes sure the correct notes come out.

In the key of B flat

B flat instruments are also called instruments *in the key of B flat* or *pitched in B flat*.

In C

There are also trumpets in other keys. C trumpets, which are most widely used in classical music, aren't transposing instruments – a C in their music produces a concert pitch C. But when you're reading music, you don't have to worry about what pitch an instrument is in, all you have to do is play the notes you see on the paper and the correct notes will come out, regardless of the pitch of the instrument – as long as you don't use an instrument in one key to read a part written for an instrument in another key.

B flat trumpet

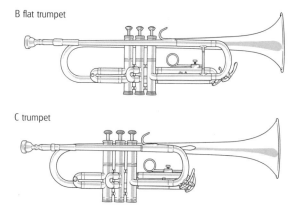

C trumpet

The shorter C trumpet sounds brighter than the B flat trumpet

Shorter and clearer

The tube of a C trumpet is just a little shorter than the tube of an 'ordinary' B flat trumpet – you can see the difference most clearly at the tuning slide and the third valve slide. The shorter tube not only makes the C trumpet sound one tone higher, it also gives the instrument a brighter and lighter timbre.

Trombones

Trombones are pitched in B flat, in that when the slide is in the first (closed) position, only the B flat harmonic series can be played. However, the trombone is not a transposing instrument, as trombonists do not play transposed parts – when they read a B flat, they produce a concert pitch B flat. However, in brass band music, the trombone is treated as a transposing instrument – it is written a whole tone higher than it sounds just like a B flat trumpet.

Other pitches

Trombones, trumpets, cornets and flugelhorns come in other pitches too. For instance, if you play a C on an *E flat cornet*, you'll hear a concert pitch E flat. If you want to know more about these instruments, turn to Chapter 11, *The Family*.

Rough Guide to Reading Music

You can read more about transposing instruments and transposing in Chapter 16 of *The Rough Guide to Reading Music and Basic Theory*.

3. LEARNING TO PLAY

How hard is it to learn to play? Do you have to take lessons? Do you need to practise for hours every day? This chapter discusses these and other questions you may have about learning to play a brass instrument.

It's not very hard to walk up to a piano and play a C, or any other note, even if you've never played before. All you have to do is to press the correct key. But with the trumpet it's not so simple.

Make your own notes

A trumpet doesn't have a key or button for each note. You have to make the note yourself, using just three valves, the tension of your lips and the way you blow – and learning how to do so can take a while. In time, you'll learn to hear the note you want to play in your head before you play it; this helps you always to hit the correct note and reduces the chance of 'splitting' notes.

Which note?

On most instruments you can tell which note you're playing by looking at what you're doing with your hands. But on a brass instrument – as with singing – you have to learn to *hear* which note you're producing.

Breath control

Your lips and the way you blow not only determine what note you play, but also how it sounds and whether it's in tune straight away. To be able to play long phrases, in tune and with a good tone, you need to develop proper breath control. If you try to play a long, sustained note the first time you pick up a brass instrument you'll probably feel dizzy and light-headed. Learning how to control your breath cures this problem.

Embouchure

You also need to develop a good *embouchure*. This French term describes the position and use of the lips and tongue, and all the muscles around them. Brass players often use the word 'lip' to mean the same thing. It takes time to develop a good embouchure, though some people have the advantage of a mouth shape that's naturally suited to the instrument they play.

Taking lessons

You need to have a good teacher if you are to develop good embouchure and breath control from the start. You can learn to play without a teacher, whatever the instrument, but if you teach yourself bad habits it will often take a long time to unlearn them.

Other advantages

You'll learn other things too if you take lessons, such as a good posture, so that you don't get sore arms, shoulders or neck.

Reading music

If you take lessons you'll probably also learn to read music. It's true that loads of people have learnt to play their instrument without reading music, but it is an incredibly useful skill. Here are some of the advantages:

- It gives you the freedom to turn up and play along with a group, even if you don't know the music.
- It gives you access to millions of pieces of sheet music and practice material.
- It allows you to write down pieces for yourself or parts for other musicians.
- It gives you a better understanding of what you're playing.
- It's essential if you want to play in an orchestra, brass band or wind band.

Group and individual tuition

While most people take individual lessons, you could also

opt for group tuition if it's available in your area. Personal tuition is more expensive – expect to pay around £15–30/$20–50 per hour – but it can be tailored exactly to your needs.

Music schools
You may also want to check whether there are any music schools or teachers' collectives in your vicinity. These often offer good-value lessons (although in the UK they are not as subsidized as they used to be) as well as bonuses such as ensembles to play in and masterclasses.

Ask first
If you are inquiring about a music school or a teacher, don't just find out what it will cost. Here are a few more things you may want to ask:
- Is a trial lesson included? This will give you a chance to see if you get on with the teacher – and with the instrument.
- Is the teacher still interested in taking you on as a student if you are just doing it for the fun of it, or are you expected to practise for hours every day?
- Will you have to buy a whole stack of books or will the teaching materials be provided?
- Is the teacher familiar with the style of music you want to play, and will you be required to learn other styles?
- Can the teacher offer advice on purchasing an instrument?
- Can you record the lessons, so that you can play them back at home?

Looking for a teacher
Music stores often have private teachers on staff, or they can refer you to one. You could also ask your local Musician's Union, or a music teacher at a high school or music college in your area. Also check the classified ads in newspapers and music magazines and try the *Yellow Pages*.

Trumpet, flugelhorn or cornet?
The trumpet, flugelhorn and cornet are very similar instruments, so which should you learn? The cornet is often regarded as the easiest instrument for beginners. Some players find it easier to blow than a trumpet or flugelhorn, and it's also quite small, which makes it easier for young players to hold properly.

Switching instruments

There are countless players who play more than one of these instruments – it's relatively easy to switch from one to another. The biggest difference is between the trumpet and flugelhorn, but many musicians play both.

The trombone

The trombone is a big instrument with a big mouthpiece, and it takes quite a lot of breath to play it. This makes the trombone difficult for small children, as does the fact that you need quite long arms to fully extend the slide.

Alto trombones

For this reason, some teachers start small children off on an *alto trombone*, which is a size smaller, and move them on to a tenor trombone later. It can take a while to adjust to the slide positions of the tenor instrument, but the transition isn't that difficult.

Small children occasionally start off on the smaller alto trombone

Other solutions

Some teachers start young trombonists on a normal-sized trombone, but don't get them to play in the sixth or seventh positions until they have grown a little. Others favour using a special extension piece (available from some music shops), which allows short arms to reach these positions.

Teeth and braces

When children loose their milk teeth, there's no need for them to stop playing, whatever brass instrument they play. Braces can cause problems, though these can sometimes be rectified by getting a mouthpiece that doesn't press the inside of the lip against the metal on the teeth. Special brace guards and dental wax can also be purchased.

Left-handed

Some players, of course, are left-handed, but most of them

play on ordinary 'right-handed' instruments. There are some left-handed instruments on sale, but the choice is very limited. If you have a trombone, you can simply assemble it the other way round.

PRACTISING

The first time you ever play a trumpet or a trombone, your lips will start to hurt after just a few minutes. The discomfort will only lessen once you develop your embouchure, and the best way to do that is to play as often as possible. If you don't play for a week, you'll feel it at once when you pick up the instrument again.

Half an hour

It's better to practise half an hour every day than a full afternoon each week. That's true of every instrument, but it applies especially to the instruments covered in this book.

Your ear

As a brass player, you also need to train your ear, to make sure every note you play is in tune. At first you may find it difficult to tell what's in tune and what's not, but it gets easier the longer you've been playing.

CDs and tapes

A lot of practice books – in all styles of music – come with a CD or tape of examples to illustrate points in the text or to play along to. This can be very instructive as well as making practising more enjoyable.

Keeping time

All musicians should be able to keep time, not only drummers and conductors. For this reason, it's good to practise with a metronome – at least once in a while. This small device ticks or beeps out a steady adjustable pulse, helping you to work at tempo, timing and rhythm skills.

Electronics and computers

A drum machine can be a good alternative to a metronome – it does the same job but can give you a drumbeat to play along to. There are similar machines that can be programmed to play bass lines and simple harmonies too, and

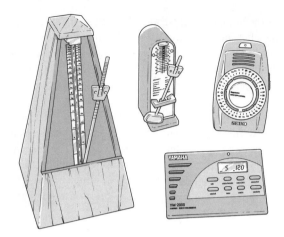

Two mechanical (wind-up) metronomes and two electronic ones

even machines as well as computer software that offer you an entire electronic band to play along to. If you want to be able to play music that you've heard on a recording, a *phrase trainer* (or equivalent computer software) could be useful. This is a device that can slow down a musical phrase from a CD or other source so you can figure it out at your own speed.

Keep playing
The two best ways to learn how to play? Play as much as you can, whether alone or in a band, and go out to see other musicians play. Whether they are living legends or local amateurs, you can learn something from every gig or concert.

THE NEIGHBOURS
Trumpet-like instruments have for centuries been used to wake soldiers – partly because they can be played very loudly and the sound carries extremely well. This does have some obvious drawbacks – so here are a few tips to help you practise without disturbing everyone in the vicinity.

Practice mute
A practice mute is a kind of cone that you stick into the bell of your instrument. The mute closes off the bell, apart from one or more tiny holes, which allow very little sound

to come through. This massively reduces the sound, so that only people in the same room will hear you playing. However, when using a practice mute you need to blow a bit harder, and the pitch goes up slightly, so you have to adjust your playing when you start or stop using it. For this reason it's not a good idea to practise routinely with this kind of mute (or the two types of practice mutes explained below). Prices for practice mutes start at around £20/$30.

A practice mute

Peacemaker

The *Peacemaker* is a mute which blows the muted sound straight into your ears through plastic tubes and earplugs, so you can hear what you are doing better.

Silent Brass

The Yamaha *Silent Brass* mute goes a step further. It's a plastic mute with a small built-in microphone, which is attached to an amplifier the size of a personal stereo and a pair of headphones. You can use the amp to add some reverb to the sound, making it seem a bit more 'real'. And you can connect other devices to the amp, such as a tape or CD player to play along to, a keyboard, or another *Silent Brass*. The price is around £150/$250.

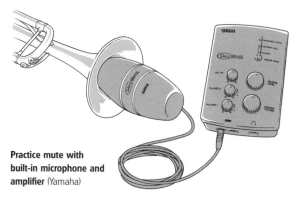

Practice mute with built-in microphone and amplifier (Yamaha)

Brass short cut mute

To practise your embouchure you can also get a *brass short cut mute*: a metal pipe with a small bell at one end and your mouthpiece at the other. You can practise just using your mouthpiece, but this mute makes it sound a bit better.

Simply playing

In the end, you will learn more and enjoy playing more without practice mutes. It may help to keep your neighbours happy if you agree practice times with them, and it'll cost you nothing. If that doesn't work, you could consider trying to soundproof a small room or part of a room. There are books available on sound insulation.

Protect your ears

If you play with a loud band you should consider protecting your ears. Simple earplugs make it difficult to play, because they simply bung up your ears, but you can get more expensive protectors which allow you to hear what's being played whilst making everything a bit less loud.

4. BUYING BRASS

Because they are not all that complicated, you can buy a decent trumpet, trombone, flugelhorn or cornet at an affordable price. This chapter will give you an idea of what everything costs and the best places to go to buy an instrument, new or second-hand. Chapter 5 has tips on choosing the best instrument you can afford.

You can get a brand-new trumpet from as little as £200/ $300, and that includes a mouthpiece and a case, although a reliable instrument that will play easily and in tune for a good few years will set you back some £350/$500 or more. Most professional trumpets cost at least £1500/$2000, and there are even instruments that cost five times as much – but they are very rare.

Flugelhorns, cornets and trombones
The prices of flugelhorns, cornets and trombones start at around £300/$400. For the very best you will pay roughly the same as for a top-quality trumpet. You can pay even more than that, if you want a specialist instrument like a hand-made, silver-plated bass trombone.

Looking and playing
Professional instruments look pretty much the same as the very cheapest models. To *see* the differences you need to take a close look. To *hear* the differences you need to be a fairly experienced player. Here are some of those differences.

More time
Compared to cheaper models, more time and care is

devoted to the making of expensive instruments, so that they sound better, and so that the moving parts slide more smoothly and last longer. More work is done by hand, from hammering the bell to making sure the valves slide perfectly. With the very cheapest instruments, there is more chance that something will break, and if it does it may well be more difficult to repair.

More expensive materials

For a higher price you may also get better brass, a bell made of special metal, or a silver-plated or even gold-plated (*gilded*) instrument.

More choice

Usually, the more you spend, the more choice you have. You may be able to choose from different leadpipes, tuning slides and bells, for instance, so that you can precisely tailor your instrument to the way you play and the sound you want. Some brands offer as many as fifty versions of a single type of trumpet.

Better value

Whether you are buying an expensive instrument or an affordable one, one thing is certain: you will get more value for money today than you did a few years ago. All the same, there are still trumpets around that aren't worth the money, especially in the very lowest price range – some will never play in tune, while others will never have a smooth piston action or produce a good tone. But these instruments are the exceptions.

Another player

To hear how good an instrument is, you need to be able to play quite well. That's unlikely to be the case if you're buying your first one. So if possible take someone with you who can play, or go to a shop where one of the salespeople plays your instrument.

Never

The most important advice is never to buy an instrument without hearing it first. In a good shop you will be given all the time you need to try out a couple. You can read about what to listen out for in the next chapter.

THE SHOP

You're always best off buying your instrument in a shop where the staff really know what they're talking about. Then you can be pretty certain that you'll end up with an instrument which has nothing wrong with it, and which will give you years of enjoyment – new or second-hand.

Fast repairs

If you buy an instrument in a shop which carries out its own repairs, then you can return the instrument if anything goes wrong with it, and you're likely to get it back pretty quickly.

Renting

Some shops rent instruments as well as selling them. The price is often around £25/$35 per month although it can vary greatly. Many shops have a 'rent-to-own' option, which is a great way to find out whether you definitely want to play an instrument. You hire it as normal and if within a few months you decide to buy it, the money you've spent on renting it is deducted from the price. There are also shops that will let you exchange a second-hand instrument you bought there for another if you decide you don't like it.

Second-hand

A used brass instrument normally costs around half of its original price. For that amount it should be in good condition, with no dents, rust, holes or other damage.

Shop or private sale?

Purchasing a used instrument privately, from an ad in the paper, for example, is usually cheaper than buying the same instrument from a shop. However, shops do have their advantages. As well as having a selection of instruments to choose from, you can go back if you have any questions or problems, and you're likely to get a guarantee. Also, good dealers tend not to ask outrageous prices, whereas private sellers sometimes do – either because they don't know any better, or because they think you don't.

An informed opinion

If you buy second-hand, it's even more important to take

someone with you who knows what they're talking about – especially if you're going to check out an instrument at someone's home.

Valuation

If you want to be really sure whether a used instrument is worth the money, get it valued. A good shop can give you an appraisal, and they'll also tell you whether the instrument needs any work doing and what it will cost. You can read technical tips about second-hand instruments on page 56 and onwards.

The player

Two musicians can make entirely different sounds on the same instrument – don't think that if you buy the model used by your favourite player you'll make the same tone. Certainly the instrument is important, but it's the player who really determines the sound.

Brochures and magazines

If you want to know what's on the market, get hold of as many brochures as you can find. But remember to get a price list to go with each – the brochures are designed to make you spend more than you probably need to. There are also special magazines on sale which review instruments and mouthpieces, and there's lots more info on the Internet. More about these and other resources can be found on pages 126–127.

Trade fairs

One last tip: if a music trade fair or convention is being held anywhere near you, go and check it out. Besides being able to try out and compare a considerable number of instruments, you will also have the chance to meet plenty of product specialists, as well as numerous fellow players – who can be a great source of independent advice.

5. A GOOD INSTRUMENT

Trumpets come lacquered or plated, with various bells and bores, with rings or triggers, and with a selection of water keys, tuning slides and other options. And the same goes for trombones, flugelhorns and cornets. This chapter explains how the specifications affect sound and playability, and tells you what to look and listen for when you're trying out instruments. Mouthpieces are covered in Chapter 6.

The first and longest section of this chapter is about the different parts of an instrument and how each affects the overall tone and feel. If you'd prefer to choose an instrument using just your ears, then turn to page 53.

Brass
Brass is a metal alloy made of a lot of copper, quite a bit of zinc and small amounts of a few other metals.

Lacquered
Bare, untreated brass makes your hands smell and quickly becomes dull. For these reasons it is usually finished with a clear lacquer, or with a lacquer with a very slight golden tint. The lacquer is usually high-gloss but there are also instruments with a matt finish.

Silver plating
Silver-plated instruments last longer than lacquered ones, but you have to polish them more often and they cost more. On a trumpet, the difference will be between around £50–150/$75–200.

The sound

Lacquer is much thicker than silver plate, which is why lacquered instruments are often said to sound a little warmer, smoother and less bright – the lacquer is supposed to mute the sound a little. Does that mean you'll be able to hear the difference? In most cases hardly or not at all.

Gold plating

The extra money you can spend on a gold-plated instrument buys you a sound which can be described as a little richer. If only the valve caps are gold-plated, or the inside of the bell, you are unlikely to be able to hear the difference.

Nickel

Nickel-plated trumpets, which are said to sound a little less expressive, are rare nowadays. Some parts are still nickel-plated, though. Nickel has a slightly 'harder' shine than silver, it costs less, lasts a long time and is easy to maintain, but many people are allergic to it.

Different looks

Sometimes you'll see three types of metal on one instrument – a basic yellow brass instrument with a slightly reddish-looking gold brass bell and nickel-plated slides, for example. Coloured instruments, available in black, red, blue and other colours, are quite popular in the US.

BELL MATERIAL

Quite often the bell will be a slightly different colour to the rest of the instrument, indicating that a different material has been used for its specific sound, such as a brass containing more copper. On expensive instruments you can often choose between several different bells.

Darker, warmer and redder

Generally, the more copper the brass contains, the darker and warmer the resulting sound and the redder the colour. An instrument with a high-copper bell also responds slightly more easily, according to many players.

Gold brass and red brass

'Ordinary' brass, with a yellowish hue, contains somewhere

between sixty and seventy percent copper, and is also known as *yellow brass*. There are several names for brass with extra copper, such as *gold brass* and *rose brass*, whilst alloys with especially high copper content are often referred to as *red brass*. Whether you pay more for extra copper varies from one brand to the next.

Silver, bronze or glass

There are also bells made of other materials. For instance, a bell made of solid silver or bronze supposedly gives you a much brighter sound, and there are even trumpets with bells made of glass.

Engraving

The brand name is virtually always engraved into the bell, sometimes with all kinds of decorations around it. With some brands you can choose from different engravings – if you're prepared to pay a bit more.

THE BORE

If you pinch the end of a garden hose, you get a hard, 'sharp' jet of water. Wind instruments work in much the same way – the narrower a tube is, the more penetrating and piercing the sound becomes. The diameter and shape of the tube is called the *bore*.

Diameter

Brochures usually tell you the size of an instrument's bore, the figure given being the width of the tube at the valves. For a trumpet with a large bore that number is usually about 0.460" (11.7mm) or more, whilst for one with a small bore it will be around 0.450" (11.4mm) or less. Those differences don't look very big on paper, but they make a lot of difference when you play.

Medium-sized

In order to play a trumpet with a large bore, you need a good embouchure and good breath control. A very small bore demands experience too. If you are just beginning, you're usually best off with a medium-sized bore (about 0.455"). On a flugelhorn, a medium-sized bore is smaller (about 0.450").

Different sounds

A trumpet with a small bore gives a brighter, lighter and more piercing sound. An instrument with a larger bore sounds bigger and broader, a little more mellow and warm. As you might expect, the bigger the bore, the easier it is to play low notes, whilst a small bore makes it easier to play very high notes.

Other differences

With a larger bore you can generally produce more volume. It's also slightly easier to colour the note, and the sound blends more easily with other instruments. That's one reason why you are most likely to come across large-bore instruments in a symphony orchestra. With a smaller bore it's a little easier to play in tune, whilst playing very loud is difficult. Small-bore instruments sound more focused and give more attack, and are often favoured by jazz musicians.

How big?

Some manufacturers indicate the bore with figures, others use words like small, medium and large, but be aware that 'large' does not mean the same for every brand. If a brochure does give figures, they are likely to be in inches (multiply by 25.4 to convert to mm; a 0.460" bore size is 0.460 x 25.4 = 11.68 mm).

Trombone

Trombonists often start on an instrument with a small bore: after all, even a 'small-bore' trombone is a good deal wider than a large-bore trumpet. Trombones often have standard bore sizes. The narrowest trombones have a bore of 0.490" (12.45 mm) whilst the widest measure 0.547" at the same point. Bass trombones are a little wider still (0.562").

Dual-bore trombones...

Some trombones have a *dual bore*. That means that the first inner tube of the slide (the *upper slide tube*) is less wide than the second (the *lower slide tube*). A much-used combination is 0.525"/0.547". The narrower upper tube makes blowing a little easier, whilst the wider lower tube gives you the bigger sound of a wider-bore instrument.

The fact that the lower slide tube is wider than the upper one also makes the sound a little warmer or mellower. Dual-bore trombones are sometimes used as an intermediate step between a small- and large-bore instrument.

...and trumpets

On dual-bore trumpets, the tube may be noticeably narrower at the start of the tuning slide than it is at the valves.

Shape

Two instruments which are advertised as having the same bore may nonetheless sound and play very differently – they may have similar bores at the points where they are measured but different bores if you look at the entire instrument, from the leadpipe to the rim of the bell. Such differences are very hard if not impossible to see. But you can hear them and feel them. According to most experts, the shape of the bore is actually more important than the exact bore diameter at the valves.

Less conical

American flugelhorns, for example, often sound a little edgier or less mellow than flugelhorns made in Europe. The reason is that the American type starts wider and finishes less wide than the European model. So the difference between narrow (at the mouthpiece) and wide (at the bell) is smaller – the American flugelhorn is less *conical*.

THE BELL

In brochures, you will quite often come across the term *wire-reinforced rim*. This sounds more impressive than it actually is, because the rim of the bell is reinforced by a thick metal *bell wire* on just about every instrument. The size of the instrument at the rim is called the *bell size*, and it naturally has an effect on the sound – as does the shape of the bell.

Sizes

The bell of a trumpet or cornet is usually no bigger than 5" (12.7cm) in diameter, while a flugelhorn bell will be around 6" (15.2cm). Trombones start at 7.5" (19cm) and bass trombones may have 10" bells (over 25cm).

Shape

Some bells only flare completely towards the end, whilst on other models the flare begins sooner. The exact shape isn't always easy to see, but you can hear and feel it when you play – the earlier the bell flares, the more it behaves like a larger bell.

Large or small

As with the rest of the instrument, the larger and more conical the bore of the bell (the sooner the tube begins to flare), the easier it will be to play low notes and the broader the instrument will sound. In their professional series, some brands offer many different bells, each with a different bore, for the same trumpet.

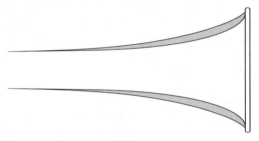

The sooner a bell begins to flare, the broader the sound can be

One-piece bells

Most expensive instruments have a *one-piece bell* – a bell made out of a single piece of brass (see Chapter 12, *How They're Made*). It's cheaper to make a bell out of two pieces, but the seam where the metal is joined can make the sound a little bit less bright, so a one-piece bell is preferable. One-piece bells are also described as *solid bells* or *seamless bells.*

Tuning with your bell

Some expensive trumpets can be tuned with the bell. An instrument with a *tuning bell* or *tuneable bell* can be 'stretched' or 'shortened' at a point just beyond the third valve, before the last bend. Supporters of tuneable bells say they give you a better tone, because the tube is not inter-rupted by an adjustable tuning slide, whilst critics say they don't tune properly. To keep everybody happy there are trumpets with both a tuneable bell and a tuning slide.

Different bells

If you can tune with the bell, you can also remove it, which means you can use various bells as and when you desire. One for a slightly warm sound, for example, and another for something brighter.

A flick

You may sometimes see a player flicking a fingernail against the bell of an instrument to hear what sound it makes. Supposedly, you can tell a lot about how the whole instrument sounds this way. Others disagree, pointing out that there are awful trumpets with bells that sound great, and just as many fine instruments with bells that don't sound good at all.

THE LEADPIPE

You hear less about leadpipes than about bells because the differences are smaller and harder to see. But there are differences – some instruments even have interchangeable leadpipes.

Flare

The leadpipe of a trumpet, for instance, can flare more or less quickly from mouthpiece to tuning slide, or it can be a little narrower or wider overall. The more the leadpipe flares or the wider it is, the more the instrument will sound like one with a larger bore. That isn't the only variation – you can also get *multi-tapered leadpipes*, with various tapers along their length.

Three choices

On some trumpets you can choose from two, three or more different leadpipes. You need to make that choice in advance, because you can't change them yourself. On trombones you usually can.

Material

The material which the leadpipe is made of is not very important to the sound, but it does affect how long the leadpipe will last. For example, brass with extra copper, such as rose brass, is less prone to the corrosive effect of saliva and dirt than brass with less copper in it.

Reversed leadpipe

On a trumpet with a *reversed leadpipe*, the tuning slide doesn't slide into the leadpipe but over it. As a result, the air column in the instrument is disturbed by the small rim between the two sections approximately 4 inches (10cm) further from the mouthpiece, and this can help produce a smoother tone.

Easier to play

Some players find a trumpet with a reversed leadpipe a little easier to play, or to play in tune. However, others prefer the bit more resistance provided by an ordinary leadpipe, and many players claim a reversed leadpipe has no audible effect on tuning. That's why even expensive trumpets come with or without reversed leadpipes – some brands let you choose. Models with a reversed leadpipes are available in most price ranges.

TUNING SLIDE

Tuning slides come in two basic models. One is very round, the other a little more angular. Some expensive trumpets come with one of each.

Single and dual radius

The round model is usually called a *single-radius* tuning slide, whilst the various names for the angular type include *dual-radius* and *square-bend* tuning slide. Most players consider the first type easier to play and say it sounds as it looks – rounder. With the angular design, the instrument supposedly responds a little better, and high notes are easier to hit. Not everyone agrees, of course, if only because not everyone tries the same slides on the same trumpets.

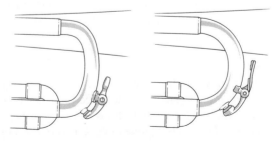

A dual-radius and a single-radius tuning slide

Two braces

Some tuning slides have one brace, some have two and some have none at all. Those braces are not only there for strength, they also contribute to the sound (see page 40).

Main tuning slide

The tuning slide is often referred to as *main tuning slide*, in order to distinguish it from the valve slides, which are used for fine-tuning only.

Trombones

The bend at the end of a trombone slide can also be angular or rounded. But the shape has less effect on the sound than that of a trumpet's tuning slide.

WATER KEYS

Most water keys are very simple keys with a spring and a small cork, but there are some small variations.

Rubber

Some models have a small piece of rubber, precisely the right shape to fill the hole of the water key, instead of a piece of cork. This way the tube is not 'interrupted' by the hole.

Amado

Other manufacturers prefer to use the Amado water key, which also stops the airflow being interrupted. It looks a little less obtrusive than the ordinary model, and because it has no cork it's less likely to leak. You do need to oil it regularly, though, otherwise there's a chance it will open but refuse to close again.

An Amado water key

None at all

Sometimes there is no water key on the third valve slide. On cheap instruments that's because it's cheaper to do without; on expensive instruments it's said to make for better sound and intonation. Either way, you have to remove the bow to let the moisture run out.

HEAVY OR LIGHT

Not all trumpets weigh the same amount. Light instruments generally have a somewhat 'lighter' sound, they are lighter to play and they respond more easily. Weight differences are mainly to do with the thickness of the tube or the bell, but there are also all kinds of other tricks to make an instrument heavier.

Heavier

Heavyweight instruments tend to have a 'heavier', thicker, richer tone than those with thin walls. They're also easier to play loudly without the sound distorting or getting edgy. You retain more control over the highest notes, and the sound is dense and focused. On the other hand, the heavier an instrument is, the harder work it is to play it.

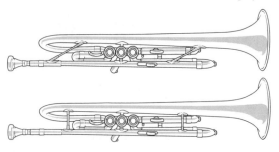

The braces between the leadpipe and bell may be straight or diagonal

Braces

Rather than simply using heavier tubing, instruments can also be made heavier by adding parts. For instance, some trumpets don't have a brace at the tuning slide, while others have one or two. And some models have diagonal braces, making them longer and a little heavier. Other instruments have double leadpipes (twin tubes), extra-heavy finger hooks and rings, and so on.

Heavy caps

Some trumpets can be fitted with extra-heavy *bottom valve*

caps. These 'valve weights' come in different sizes, and sometimes you get a whole set when you buy an instrument. There are many fewer such accessories for trombones, but they do exist.

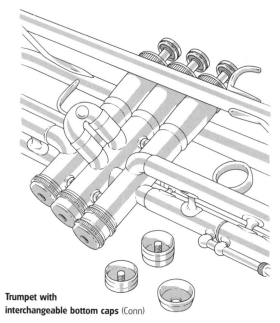

**Trumpet with
interchangeable bottom caps** (Conn)

Heavy all over

Monette, Courtois and a few other brands make extremely heavy, expensive trumpets that weigh nearly twice as much as normal instruments, with double-walled bells, extra-thick tubes and so on.

**An extra-heavy trumpet with a double-walled bell, among other
features** (Courtois Evolution)

Mouthpieces

It's not just the instrument that can be made heavier, but also the mouthpiece – see page 70.

VALVE SLIDES

On most trumpets and cornets you can fine-tune certain notes using the first and third valve slides. On most flugelhorns, only the third valve slide is adjustable. Trombonists have just one very big 'valve slide': the slide. There's more on trombone slides from page 47 onwards.

Correcting notes

Trumpets, cornets and flugelhorns all have a few notes which normally sound a little too high. Low D and low C sharp are two examples. You can lower those notes while you play by moving the third valve slide out a little. Why not simply make that tube a little longer? Because that would make other notes sound too low.

Ring

On many instruments, the third valve slide ring is adjustable, so you can move it closer towards you, or further away, as required. This feature is found especially on cheaper trumpets, because they're often used by children.

Security

Sometimes the third valve slide has a stop which prevents the slide from slipping off if you move it out too far. Some safety catch designs, as shown in the diagram, allow you to adjust the amount you can extend the slide.

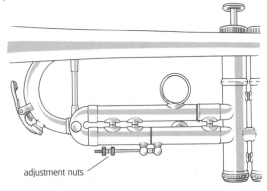

adjustment nuts

Adjustable safety catch on the third valve slide

First valve slide

Many instruments have a ring, or a hook or saddle, on the first valve slide as well, and on some models it's an option.

One of the notes you fine-tune with this slide is the low F. That's why it's occasionally referred to as call the *F-valve slide,* just as the third valve slide is sometimes called the *D-valve slide* or *C♯-valve slide.*

No slide

Some players think that you shouldn't use the first valve slide to fine-tune, saying it's better to 'lip it in' – to adjust the tuning with your embouchure. There's no best solution, so it's best to let your teacher advise you on this if you haven't been playing very long.

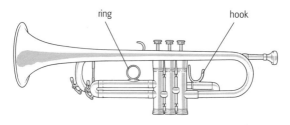

ring   hook

A ring on the third valve slide, a hook or saddle on the first

Second valve slide

The second valve slide is so short that you can't use it for fine-tuning. It does usually have a small 'button', to make it easier to pull out when cleaning the instrument.

Triggers

Flugelhorn tuning slides have so-called triggers (see pages 11–12). Usually, it's only the third valve slide that has such a mechanism – a flugelhorn's conical shape makes it easier to fine-tune with your embouchure than a trumpet. The number of triggers doesn't tell you anything about the price or the quality of an instrument: there are professional flugelhorns with no triggers at all and cheap ones which have two.

Trumpet triggers

Some trumpeters also prefer to work with a trigger instead of a ring or a hook – especially on the first valve slide, which can be a little difficult to shift using your thumb. You can have a trigger fitted to your instrument for around £100–150/$150–200.

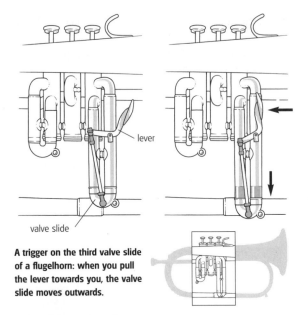

A trigger on the third valve slide of a flugelhorn: when you pull the lever towards you, the valve slide moves outwards.

Valve slide or trigger?
Confusingly, some trumpeters call the ordinary moveable valve slide a trigger – but this isn't technically correct.

Smooth
Whatever you call them, the valve slides should be able to move smoothly, without doing so of their own accord. Of course you can only test this if they are properly greased (see page 92).

VALVES
Basically, there are two types of valves: the ones you see on most trumpets, cornets and flugelhorns, and the *rotary valve* or *rotor* which you find on trombones and some trumpets.

Piston and Périnet
The first type is called the *piston valve* (see page 8) or *Périnet valve*, after the man who improved the original design (see page 100).

A ported tube
The piston is a tube through which three tubular holes (the *ports*, *portholes* or *coquilles*) run diagonally. If a valve is in

the 'up' position, the air will take the shortest possible path: straight through one of those ports. If you press the valve down, the air will be diverted through the second port, around the valve slide and back out through the third port. If you remove the second valve slide and press down the second valve, you can clearly see how it works.

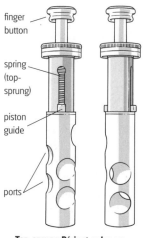

finger button

spring (top-sprung)

piston guide

ports

Top-sprung Périnet valve or piston valve

Top or bottom

In the past, Périnet valves were usually *bottom-sprung* – the spring which returns the valve to its position was below the piston, on the bottom of the valve casing. Most modern instruments are *top-sprung*; in other words, they have *top-action*. This design has the spring in a separate casing, so there is less chance that it will jump out when you remove the piston to grease it. These days, bottom-sprung or *bottom-action* valves are mainly found on low-budget trumpets and on flugelhorns.

Monel

Most instruments now have pistons made of *monel*, a metal which slides well and doesn't wear easily. If a brochure doesn't tell you the kind of material used, it will probably be something cheaper.

Smooth, silent and quick

When checking out an instrument, try the pistons for a smooth, silent and quick action, although remember that they should be oiled to function properly. If you press them down and then let them shoot upwards they should-n't rattle or rebound back down.

Breaking in

Often, the pistons only start to slide as smoothly as they should once the instrument has been played for a while: they need to be 'broken in', just like the engine of a new car. On some expensive trumpets, though, the pistons are so intensively polished (*hand-lapped*) in the factory that they slide perfectly smoothly right from the start.

Springs
Naturally, not all springs are the same. If springs feel too stiff or too light, you can have them replaced quite cheaply.

Finger buttons
Finger buttons come in different weights and thicknesses, and some have concave tops, making them feel a bit different under your fingertips. Some players fit their instruments with very light finger buttons, because that gives a slightly lighter, quicker action. Some companies also offer finger buttons with precious-stone inlays.

Rotary valves and rotary trumpets
Trumpets with rotary valves, commonly known as *rotary trumpets*, are still popular in some countries, especially Germany. Rotary valves or *cylinder valves* don't move up and down but make a rotating movement. They're somewhat more complicated than piston valves, which is one of the reasons why such trumpets are often a good deal more expensive.

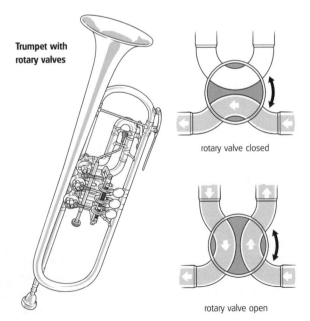

Trumpet with rotary valves

rotary valve closed

rotary valve open

Wider bores

Rotary trumpets are usually different in other ways too. For example, they have a wider bore, making for a big, powerful, warm sound. In symphony orchestras, such instruments are often used for pieces by German Romantic composers such as Brahms, and you may also see them in wind bands.

German trumpets and jazz trumpets

Rotary trumpets are also known as *German trumpets*. Conversely, in Germany, trumpets with piston valves are sometimes called *jazz trumpets*.

Playing

In order to find a good instrument, you must of course play it first. You can find testing tips from page 52 onwards.

TROMBONES

Most tenor trombones only have a slide, but some also have a single rotary valve or rotor, which expands the range of the instrument. Bass trombones have two rotary valves, and there are even trombones with three piston valves (like a trumpet) and no slide at all.

Stockings

If you take a close look at the ends of the inner slide of a trombone, you'll find that they are slightly thicker than the rest. When you move the slide, the outer slide moves over these *stockings* rather than sliding over the entire tubing length. This reduces resistance and makes sliding easier.

Materials

The outer slide is often made of a different material from that of the inner slide. Nickel silver on the inside and brass on the outside, for instance. Again, this is to make the slide action as smooth possible, and to prevent corrosion.

Lightweight

On some trombones you can opt for a special lightweight slide. For an extra £50/$75 or more, your trombone will then feel a little lighter and respond a little more easily. A few brands offer a *narrow slide*, which is also a little lighter to play.

Different slide

If a trombone sounds good but doesn't slide smoothly, try the slide of an identical instrument – it may work better.

Barrels

There is sometimes a spring in the *receiver barrels* into which the slide falls, rather than cork. This spring allows you to pull the slide towards you a little further in the first position, and some trombonists use that difference to make certain notes sound a little higher. Spring-loaded receiver barrels are known as *spring barrels*, the others as *cork barrels*.

The gooseneck

Halfway along the *gooseneck*, the first piece of tubing of the bell, there is almost always a slight curve. This makes the slide point downwards a little – more on some brands and models than others. The main purpose of this kink is to maintain the balance of the instrument. With some brands you can choose between goosenecks with different bores.

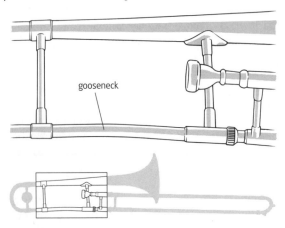

The gooseneck nearly always has a slight curve

Large bend

Jupiter is the only brand which also makes a trombone with a much larger bend in the gooseneck. The idea is that it fits more comfortably around your neck. Moreover, this trombone, which is designed especially with children in mind, has a shorter slide, a special grip for your left hand and an adjustable rest for your left thumb.

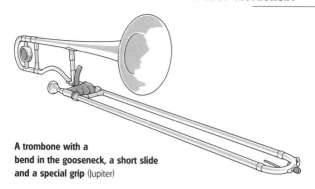

A trombone with a
bend in the gooseneck, a short slide
and a special grip (Jupiter)

Finger rings

A useful feature for small hands is a ring on the inner slide
brace. You put your first finger through the ring, instead of
resting the top of that finger against the mouthpiece or the
leadpipe.

F-attachments

A trombone has virtually the same range as a trumpet, but
one octave lower. But there are also trombones which can
go a little lower still, with a rotary valve (see pages 46–47)
and an extra piece of tubing in the bell section. When you
use the rotor the extra tubing makes the instrument longer.
The B flat in the first position then becomes an F, hence
the name *F-attachment* for the extra tubing and rotor.

Other positions

An F-attachment not only allows you to play lower notes;
you can also play a large number of the existing notes in
new positions. That can make playing trills and fast tran-
sitions easier. For a tenor trombone with an F-attachment
you should expect to pay an extra £200/$300 or more, the
amount varying widely between brands.

Open and traditional

The extra tubing which goes with an F-attachment can
either stick out some way behind the tuning slide or be
completely curled up inside the main tube. The first solution is called *open wrap*, the second *traditional* or *closed
wrap*. An open wrap has fewer sharp bends, which makes
the difference between playing with or without the F-
attachment less pronounced, and makes blowing easier.
On the other hand, it's easier to knock into things with an

open wrap, because the tube sticks out a few inches further behind you. There are also all kinds of variations on these *F-wraps*.

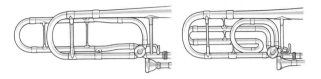

Trombones with F-attachments: an open wrap on the left and a traditional wrap on the right

Convertible and straight trombones

On a *convertible trombone* you can take the whole F-attachment or *F-section* off if you don't need it. Incidentally, trombones without an F-attachment are sometimes referred to as *straight trombones*.

Bass trombones

A bass trombone is basically the same size as a tenor trombone, but the tube is a little wider and the bell a little bigger, making the lowest notes easier to play. What's more, nearly all bass trombones have two rotary valves: the first is the F-attachment that was mentioned before, and the second adds another piece of tubing to the instrument, lowering the pitch even more.

Dependent and independent

There are two types of valve systems for bass trombones. With the *dependent* (or *offset* or *stacked*) system, which is found on most older instruments, when you use the second rotor you automatically use the first too. With the newer *inline* or *independent* system you can use both rotors independently. Using both valves together with either system will produce, in first position, either an E flat or a D depending on the length of the second rotor tube (which is why the second rotor is often called the *E flat* or *D attachment*). Using the second valve only, on an independent system, gives a G or a G flat. Thus a catalogue may list a bass trombone with an inline system as being 'B flat/F/G' or 'B flat/F/G flat'. Some brands offer interchangeable tubes for the second rotor.

Metal and string actions

The rotors are either worked by a metal *ball-and-socket* transmission between the lever and the rotor, or by a string – a system known as *string rotor action, string action* or *string F valve linkage*. A string is cheaper and there is less chance of rattling. Moreover, the lever often has a shorter stroke and it's fairly easy to adjust the mechanism yourself. On the other hand, a string can break or come loose. A good, properly adjusted mechanism with a metal transmission is more expensive but just as quiet. As you'd expect, not all trombonists agree about which is best. Depending on the brand, you may be able to choose for yourself whether you have string or metal.

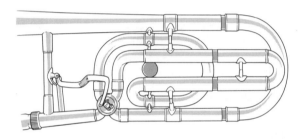

An F-attachment with a string action

Testing

If you are play-testing a trombone with rotors, feel how smoothly they work, listen to make sure they don't rattle when you let go of the lever, check how far the lever has to travel and whether that distance is adjustable, and compare how the trombone plays with and without rotors. Using the rotor(s) usually increases the resistance of the instrument, as well as influencing the tone.

With or without rotors

Every trombone plays differently with rotors and without. Not only are you adding a considerable length of tubing when you use the rotors, but the air also needs to travel around lots of extra bends.

New designs

In order to make the difference between playing with and without rotors as small as possible, all kinds of new rotor types have been devised with gentler bends. Two well-known names are Thayer and Hagmann. Some brands offer a choice between these new types and traditional rotary valves. Other manufacturers design their own systems, such as the Rotax by Willson and the CL2000 by Conn.

Valve trombones

A *valve trombone* is something quite different: a trombone with three piston valves instead of a slide. Most brands only have one model in their catalogue. If you play the trumpet, it's fairly easy to learn the valve trombone as the fingering will be familiar, though it can take a long time to get used to the longer tube and bigger mouthpiece.

A valve trombone: no slide, three piston valves

TUNING

Even the finest-sounding instrument is worthless if you can't play it in tune. Unfortunately, trumpets, cornets and flugelhorns are never completely in tune, and trombones have their deviations as well.

Adjust as you play

On trumpets, cornets and flugelhorns, the low D and the low C sharp or D flat are always a little too high. To make sure they sound in tune, you use your valve slides, your embouchure, or both.

Intonation

The better the craftsmanship on an instrument, the less you need to adjust it and the easier it is to play in tune. An instrument like that has better *intonation*, in technical terms.

The wrong side

Every manufacturer has its own ideas about how to opti-mize the intonation of an instrument. That means every trumpet, flugelhorn or cornet has its own particular tuning deviations. If you are used to having to adjust a certain note on your trumpet and you do the same on a new instrument, that note may suddenly sound very out of tune – because the new trumpet may be naturally more in tune at that point. This is one of the reasons why it can take a while to get used to a new instrument.

Tests

There are a few tests you can do to hear how good the intonation of an instrument is. First, blow all the notes you can play without valves (the harmonics). If you can already hear deviations, it's probably better to try a different instrument. Next, play all the notes you can get with the first valve, then with the second, and so on. Another test: play the scale of B major, because there's a better-than-average chance of off-notes in that scale.

Trombones

When it comes to tuning, trombones are different – after all, you can keep making adjustments with the slide until you have the perfect note. So is there such a thing as an out-of-tune trombone? Yes: one on which the positions are not where they should be. When trying out an instrument, pay particular attention to the middle and high F, the middle D and the high B flat, which are sometimes on the low side. High notes are more likely to be out of tune than low ones, and you're more likely to hear that they are out of tune too.

A GOOD SOUND

This section contains tips on testing the individual sound of an instrument. Again, taking an experienced player with you is a good idea – they'll be in a better position to get the best sound from an instrument, especially over a large range of notes. But you should never buy an instrument without also playing it yourself.

Another player

If you get somebody else to play an instrument for you, it never sounds the same as when you play the same instrument yourself. But as long as the same person demonstrates a number of instruments, you'll be able to hear the differences. Getting someone else to play also allows you to hear what the various instruments sound like at a distance.

Your mouthpiece
When choosing an instrument, always use your own mouthpiece or one of the same brand and type. If that isn't possible, then at least try them all with the same mouthpiece – otherwise you won't be listening only to the differences between instruments, you will also be hearing the differences between mouthpieces.

Using a wall
When playing a brass instrument you always point it away from yourself, so you never get to hear exactly what your audience hears. You can get a much better idea of the sound by holding the bell right in front of a wall (or a book on a music stand for trombonists).

Briefly at first
If you have to choose between various instruments, it's often best if you only play briefly on each one. Play something simple, so that you only have to concentrate on the sound and not on the notes.

Two by two
Once you have got your decision down to a particular selection of instruments, start comparing them two by two or three by three. Choose the best, reject the worst, choose the best again, and so on. Once you have identified the instruments with the best sound and you are about to 'really' choose, play longer pieces so that you get to know the instruments better.

Where do you start?
If you have no idea where to start when you walk into a store, ask the salesperson for two instruments that sound very different. A trumpet with a particularly soft sound and another with a brilliant sound, for instance. Decide which sound you prefer and go on from there. Or try a very cheap one alongside the most expensive one they have, just to hear how much they differ.

Not the same

Not everyone agrees on what is a good sound. What one player calls 'painfully shrill', another may describe as 'beautifully bright', and what's 'warm' to one person may be 'dull' to someone else.

Styles of music

What kind of sound you prefer is purely a matter of taste, but certain sounds are especially suitable for certain styles of music. A symphony orchestra usually calls for a trumpet with a big, full sound that blends well with other instruments, for example, whilst the trumpets used in salsa bands often have a more piercing tone to cut through the rest of the group.

Response

An instrument must have a good response: notes must speak easily and consistently. Try the response with loud and soft notes, from high to low. If you can still hear a trumpet at the back of a hall when it's playing the softest notes, it has good projection too.

Loud or soft

An instrument doesn't just sound louder when you blow harder, it also sounds different – more brilliant or edgy, ideally. But the difference should not be too large. For instance, some instruments may sound muddy, dull or unclear when you play very softly or very low, or both. Or they may become very shrill and thin when you play loudly or when you play high notes. When playing the entire range of the instrument, loud or soft, the changes should be very gradual, and even the loudest tones should not break up or distort.

Trombones

If you are trying out a trombone with an F-attachment, do all the playing tests with and without it. The unavoidable difference should be as small as possible. Trombones have two problem high notes – the high A flat and the highest D – which tend to come out less than evenly.

Small differences

Even two 'identical' trumpets may still sound slightly

different – regardless of the price range. So you should always buy the instrument you played, and not the 'same instrument' from the storeroom.

SECOND-HAND

There are a lot of used instruments on sale. Not because they don't last very long (a life-span of thirty years or more is not unusual) but because many players go on to buy a better instrument after a few years. So what do you need to watch out for when you buy second-hand?

Mouthpieces

Take your own mouthpiece with you, if you have one. It's unlikely that you'll play comfortably with the mouthpiece that comes with the instrument. If you do buy a used mouthpiece, there are a few things you should pay particular attention to. First, most mouthpieces are silver-plated. If this protective layer is damaged, your lips will touch the brass below. That won't taste good, and there's a chance of getting a rash on your lips – even very small scratches can be homes for bacteria. Some players aren't too bothered: they like the extra bit of 'grip' you get with a lightly scratched mouthpiece. With or without scratches, do always clean a used mouthpiece before trying it out (see pages 63 and 94). And bear in mind that mouthpieces which aren't too badly damaged can be re-plated.

The lacquer

All instruments, but especially old ones, may have patches where the lacquer has disappeared, as a result of sweat, rubbing or both. These patches are likely to make your hands smell of brass, and where there are scratches, even tiny ones, the lacquer can peel off, causing the brass to corrode. Instruments can be re-lacquered if necessary; expect to pay around £300/$400 for a trumpet, and more for a trombone. You can get a new silver-plate finish too, for about half as much again.

The leadpipe

Take out the tuning slide and take a look through the leadpipe. It should look clean and smooth. On a flugelhorn, do the same with the tuning mouthpipe, and on a trombone you can look through the first slide tube if you take the outer slide off. An extremely dirty leadpipe can only be cleaned in a special bath (see page 97).

Spots
If there are small round patches on the leadpipe, it may be rusting from the inside. Replacing a trumpet's leadpipe can easily cost you £125/$180.

Dents
Dents – even small ones – can make the instrument play out of tune. The closer a dent is to the mouthpiece, the more of a problem it will be. A dent in the bell is less likely to affect the tuning, and will also be easier to remove.

Appraisals
Lumps of solder can be a sign of shoddy repairs. You may also come across instruments that have had parts replaced, such as a leadpipe or a bell. If you don't want to take any risks, have the instrument appraised (see page 30) before buying it.

Valves
While one player presses the valves straight down, another may push them a little to one side, making them wear slightly more in that direction. If your way of playing is very different to the previous owner's, the valves may feel stiffer to you than they ever did to that player.

Play
If you pull a valve piston up a little, out of its casing, you shouldn't be able to feel any play. If you can move it side to side, rather than just up and down, it will probably leak – and getting valves and valve casings repaired or replaced isn't cheap.

The plop test
A test to check whether the valves leak is to pull out the valve slides one by one, without pressing down the valves. You should hear a 'plopping' sound when each valve slide is removed. If you don't, there's a problem. The leak may be in the valve or in the slide: the second valve slide especially can suffer from sweaty hands, which can even cause tiny

holes in the metal. If you have trouble getting the valve slides loose, it's not necessarily serious, but do get a professional to look at them.

Water key

If you don't get a 'plop' from the third valve slide, the problem may be a leaking water key, which is easy to repair. Checking the water key is easy: blow down one end of the valve slide and close off the other end with your finger.

The finger test

Another leak test for the valves is to pull out the first tuning slide and press the first valve. Then blow through the instrument, closing off the tube the air is now coming from with a finger (don't blow too hard as you may hurt your ears). If you hear air escaping, something is leaking. Test the other valves in the same way.

Rotary valves

You can test a rotary valve in the same way. Also feel how smoothly the rotor works, and feel if there's any excessive play. Opening rotary valves requires experience and the right tools.

Rattles

Listen for rattles when playing the instrument and also when operating the valves or rotors without playing. Unwanted noises can be the result of many things, such as play, worn-out felts, loose finger buttons, broken springs and braces that have come loose.

Trombone slides

A trombone's slide should move smoothly and be completely leak-free. To check for leaks, take off the slide and remove the mouthpiece. Rest the bow of the slide on your shoe, close off both ends of the tube with your thumbs and quickly pull the inner slide upwards about ten or fifteen inches (be careful not to pull the slide too far or fast). If the outer slide stays where it is, resting on your foot, something is leaking; if it gets pulled up a little way, it's all right. Before you do this test, make sure that the water key doesn't leak: blow down one end of the outer slide while closing off the other end with your finger.

No slide lock

Slide locks are a fairly new innovation. If you are looking at an old instrument, check to see if it has one, and if it does, try it out. Some worn slide locks open themselves, and so aren't a lot of use.

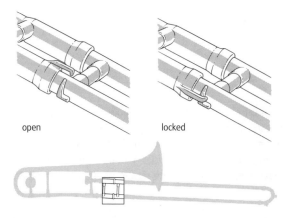

open   locked

A slide safety catch: not all older trombones have one

Serial numbers and bore

In order to find out exactly how old an instrument is, you need to know the serial number. It's usually on one of the valve casings or on the bell, next to the engraving. Lists of serial numbers and the corresponding years of manufacture for many brands can be found on the Internet (see page 127), and some shops have similar lists. A few brands also put the size of the bore on the instrument – try looking on the valve casings.

6. A GOOD MOUTHPIECE

A mouthpiece connects you to your instrument, and if it doesn't fit you properly you'll never play as well as you could. This chapter explains all the factors and measurements you should consider when choosing a mouthpiece – from cup and bore size to weighting and plating.

A mouthpiece that really suits you allows you to make a good tone with as little effort as possible. It will make it easier to learn to play, easier to produce high and low notes and easier to play in tune. And it will allow you to play for longer without losing your tone or hurting your lip.

Fit
A mouthpiece must suit your style of playing, your embouchure and everything that goes with it: from the size and tension of your lips to your lung capacity and the position of your teeth and jaws.

How they work
When you play, the rim of the mouthpiece rests against your lips. Your lips vibrate in the *cup*, the recess at the start of the mouthpiece, and you blow the vibrating air into the instrument through a small hole (the *bore* or *throat*).

Important measurements
Mouthpieces come in countless shapes and sizes. The main measurements that tell you how a mouthpiece will play and feel are:
- The size of the *bore*: the smallest opening of the mouthpiece.

- The size and contour of the *rim*: the edge that you touch with your lips.
- The diameter and depth of the *cup*.
- The *backbore*: the shape of the inside of the *shank*.

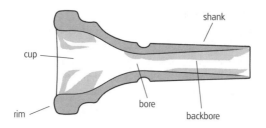

Medium mouthpieces

Many players start out on a 'medium' mouthpiece: one with a medium-sized rim, cup and bore. Most instruments are also sold with such mouthpieces. But they are not, of course, the best solution for everybody. For lips which are soft and not too strong, a medium-sized rim is too narrow (it pinches), whilst for other lips it may be too wide (so that it gets in the way). The cup may be too small (so you don't get a good sound) or too big (so that you have to work too hard), whilst the bore can be too small (which gives a poor response) or too big (making it hard to play in tune). And these are just a few examples.

Cheaper instruments

Cheaper instruments often come with quite small mouthpieces, because they are easy to play. One of the drawbacks is that it's hard to develop a good embouchure with a mouthpiece that's too small.

Swapping or buying

When buying an instrument, some stores may allow you to exchange the mouthpiece that comes with it. If not, or if you want something completely different, expect to pay between £15/$25 and £40/$60, although there are mouthpieces which cost less and some which cost much more – you can pay over £70/$100 for a gold-plated model.

Finding the right one

A mouthpiece has all kinds of different measurements,

and as a player you have quite a few yourself. Obviously, there's no simple rule to determine which mouthpiece will suit you best. Reading this chapter will help, and so will talking to your teacher or a knowledgeable salesperson.

Your own mouthpiece

If you go out shopping for a new mouthpiece, always bring the one you're currently using. Based on its dimensions and what you want to achieve (a bigger tone, easier high notes, a more aggressive sound, or whatever) a good salesperson will be able to limit the number of mouthpieces to choose from to a handful, which will save you having to try out dozens.

The sound

Classical players often select a 'large' mouthpiece, in order to achieve a big, warm tone. If you play jazz or Latin music, you'll usually be better off with a mouthpiece with a shallow cup and a smaller bore, giving you a crisper, more brilliant sound. However, very large and very small mouthpieces tend to be used by experienced players only, as they are generally difficult to play with.

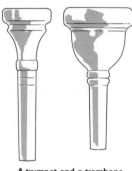

A trumpet and a trombone mouthpiece

Tiny differences

When it comes to mouthpieces, tiny changes in size are important – every hundredth of an inch counts. So when you go to buy a new mouthpiece it's best not to choose one that is a lot bigger or smaller than the one you are used to. A very different mouthpiece may seem great when you try it out, but once you've practised for a couple of hours you may find it a lot less comfortable.

Testing tips

The easiest way to select a mouthpiece, just as with instruments, is to keep comparing two or three at a time. Try three, choose the one that feels best, swap the one you like the least for another, and so on. Bear in mind that you won't get used to a different mouthpiece as easily as you would to a different instrument. Everything will feel different at first and you'll sometimes need to adapt your embouchure. That makes choosing a mouthpiece harder than it seems.

Trumpet mouthpieces

Most trumpet mouthpieces fit most trumpets – but not all of them. A long mouthpiece with a fairly thin shank may sometimes slide in so far that it touches the inner edge of the leadpipe. As a result, the mouthpiece won't fit snugly, and air may even leak out. If a mouthpiece won't go in far enough, the distance between the shank and the leadpipe edge may cause a deterioration in tone quality. The same can happen with the other instruments.

Cornet mouthpieces

Cornet mouthpieces come in two lengths. Most American (long) cornets require the long type, whilst most British (short) cornets require the short one.

Trombone mouthpieces

Trombone mouthpieces are available with a *large shank* for instruments with a bore of 0.547" or more and with a *small shank* for the smaller sizes.

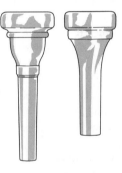

A long and a short cornet mouthpiece

Flugelhorn mouthpieces

Flugelhorn mouthpieces with a fairly narrow shank are often too thin for flugelhorns built by American brands. Sometimes this problem can be solved with a special adapter, but not always.

Disinfectant

If you are choosing mouthpieces together with a fellow player, you will minimize the risk of a rash or other complaints if you clean the mouthpieces before trying them. There are even special mouthpiece disinfectants available for the job. If one of you has a cold sore, don't exchange mouthpieces at all.

Teeth

On a completely different note, your front teeth are very important if you play a brass instrument. So it's worth telling your dentist that you play if these teeth are going to have anything done to them. There are even dentists who specialize in treating brass players.

CODES AND CATALOGUES

Mouthpieces come in hundreds of types and sizes. And the fact that just about every manufacturer has its own system to identify the different models doesn't make it any easier. For instance, the Vincent Bach 7C, the Schilke 13B and the Yamaha 11C4 are three popular trumpet mouthpieces with roughly the same dimensions and very different names. Conversely, two 5A-mouthpieces by different brands may be nothing like each other.

Cup size and depth

The only thing that all those names have in common is that the first figure tells you something about the cup diameter and the letter that follows it indicates the depth of the cup. But that doesn't help very much: with one brand, a high number means a large diameter, and on another it means a small one. Similarly, A can mean a deep or shallow cup.

Longer codes

Some mouthpieces have a longer code – such as 13A4a. In most cases the second number refers to the shape of the rim (usually between 1 and 5, from very round to very flat) and the second letter to the backbore (usually from *a* to *e*, from very narrow to very wide).

Comparable types

Next to each mouthpiece in a brochure you'll often see the names of comparable types by well-known brands. This makes life slightly easier. In addition, most brochures tell you the diameter and depth of the cup, and the shape or the width of the rim.

Descriptions

Often, brochures also offer descriptions of the characteristics of the various mouthpieces. These can offer a good starting point but they should be taken with a pinch of salt. For one thing, they tend to highlight the positive characteristics (high notes become easier...), while leaving out the negative ones (...but low notes will be much harder).

The same codes

Some brands use the same system of numbering for their trumpet, cornet and flugelhorn mouthpieces. However, that doesn't guarantee they will be similar – if you use a 5A by a particular brand for your trumpet, you won't necessarily be best off with a flugelhorn 5A by the same brand.

The differences

What exactly are the differences between deep and shallow cups, large and small bores and narrow, wide, rounded and flat rims? What will a layer of gold on a mouthpiece do for you and what difference does the weight of a mouthpiece make? All is explained in the following pages, which look at these factors one by one. You'll find a few more general mouthpiece tips on page 71–72.

THE CUP

The cup diameter is measured at the top of the inside of the cup. For trumpets and cornets, 0.59" (15mm) is a very small size, and 0.69" (17.5mm) is very large. For a tenor trombone, you can add about 0.4" (1cm) to these measurements.

Brands and measurements

The cup of a mouthpiece flares out a little at the top. The higher up you measure it, the bigger the cup diameter will appear. So two '0.60" cups' by different brands may not be exactly the same size on close inspection. For most brands a 'C' implies a medium-sized cup.

A big cup

It takes a good player to handle a mouthpiece with a very big cup size. An inexperienced player with such a mouthpiece will find it harder to play in tune, harder to jump from a high note to a low note or vice versa, and will quickly get out of breath.

A small cup

If the cup is too small, your lips will be pressed together too much. As a result, they won't be able to vibrate enough, which will make it difficult to produce a good tone. You will also be more likely to 'miss' notes. A smaller cup will often make the higher notes a little easier, but if it's too small you won't be able to play very high notes at all.

The right size

One thing that nearly everyone agrees on is that you should choose the biggest cup diameter you can handle with your embouchure.

Thick and thin lips

It's sometimes said that you need a big cup diameter if you have thick lips, and a small one if you have thin lips. This seems obvious – but lots of successful musicians have proved that it isn't always the case.

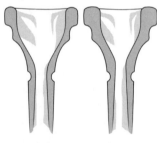

A deep, wide cup and a smaller, shallower one

Cup depth

Cups also differ in their depth. A deeper cup is harder work to play, but provides a warmer, bigger, darker tone. A shallow cup helps you produce a brighter, more focused sound and makes playing high notes easier.

Cup shape

The cup of trumpet, cornet and trombone mouthpieces is basically U-shaped on the inside, while the cup of a flugelhorn mouthpiece is more like a V. The more a cup of any mouthpiece tends towards a V-shape, the warmer, mellower and less bright the tone will be, and vice versa.

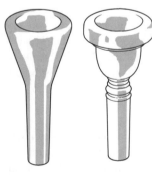

Two very similar cups on two very different mouthpieces

Cup 1, cup 2

Some brands refer to the *first cup* (the upper part of the cup) and the *second cup* (the lower part). For example, a mouthpiece may be advertised as having a relatively narrow first cup, to make high notes easier to play, and a relatively wide second cup, to ensure that the tone stays nice and broad.

THE RIM

The rim is especially important for how a mouthpiece feels: after all, it is the part which is against your lips when you play. The width is usually somewhere between 0.20" and 0.24" (5–6mm) for trumpets and around 0.04" (1mm) more for trombones.

Cushion rims

The wider the rim, the more the pressure is spread across your lips, and the less tiring the mouthpiece is to use. For this reason, wide, flat rims are sometimes called *cushion rims*. On the other hand, it's less easy to control the sound and pitch with a wide rim, and you may find high notes harder to play. If you need to take your instrument from your mouth to play large in-tervals (from very high to very low notes, or vice versa), there's a good chance that your rim is too wide.

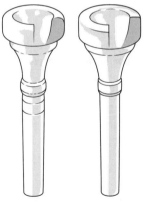

Wide and flat, narrow and rounded

With thick, soft lips you are more likely to need a wide, flat rim. A rim that is too narrow will pinch your lips and constrict their move-ments, and one that is nar-row and rounded will also feel sharper, so you won't be

A fairly rounded and a fairly flat rim

able to play for as long. However, with a narrow, rounded rim it's much easier to go from one note to the next, even in big steps, and it's easier to hit the high notes. You'll also get a bigger range.

Rim bite

Even the shape of the inner edge (*rim bite*) makes a difference. The sharper the rim bite is, the more easily an instrument will respond and the easier it will be to play in tune, but the harder it is to slide from note to note and play for a long time. A rim bite which is too 'blunt' and rounded will feel more comfortable, but creating notes with real attack and playing in tune can be difficult, and there's even a chance that air and saliva will escape while you play.

The highest point

Some mouthpieces feel bigger or smaller than they really are, because of the position of the highest point of the rim. This may be more towards the outside of the rim, making the mouthpiece feel bigger than it actually is, or more towards the inside, making it feel smaller.

The same rim

Most musicians who play more than one brass instrument, such as the trumpet, cornet and flugelhorn, choose a mouthpiece with the same shape of rim for each instrument. This makes it easier to switch from one instrument to the other. If you can't find a mouthpiece with the rim you're looking for, there are specialists who can make or copy one for you.

Combination mouthpiece

So-called *combination mouthpieces* come with one rim, but several different shanks and cups. This way you can use the same rim all the time, but choose a different cup or shank for each instrument you play. You can also change your tone – if want a brighter sound, for example, for a certain room, band or piece, you just use a smaller cup than your usual one.

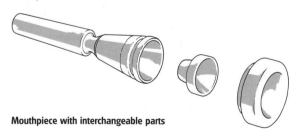

Mouthpiece with interchangeable parts

THE BORE

The bore, or throat, must be big enough to let the air pass through, while being small enough to provide you with enough resistance. Without that resistance, you won't be able to play any high notes. Basically, the size of a mouthpiece bore does much the same as the size of the instrument's bore.

Large and small bores

A bigger mouthpiece bore gives you more volume, lets you blow more freely, makes lower notes easier to play and increases your flexibility. But it requires more air and a better embouchure. A smaller bore means you can play for longer, the instrument responds better, and high notes are easier to hit. But an extremely small bore doesn't necessarily make high notes extremely easy to play – if you blow too hard down such a mouthpiece, it can suddenly feel as though it's shut off completely.

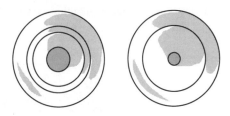

A mouthpiece with a large bore and a wide rim, and one with a small bore and a narrow rim; the opposite combination is equally possible.

Fractions of an inch

The bore of trumpet and cornet mouthpieces is generally between 0.140" and 0.160" (3.5–4mm). On flugelhorns, the latter number is an 'average' size. The bore of trombone mouthpieces lies between about 0.215" and 0.300" (5.5–7.5mm).

THE BACKBORE

Backbores come in various designs, from V-shaped to barrel-shaped, but those with a V-shape are by far the most popular. If you have a lot of air, then a slightly barrel-shaped backbore may be better for you.

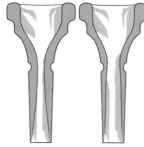

A narrow, V-shaped backbore and a wide, slightly barrel-shaped backbore

Bigger and smaller

Apart from the shape, the backbore has a similar effect to the bore: the narrower it is, the brighter the sound, and the wider it is, the darker and mellower the sound will be. If you know exactly what you have and what you want, you can go for one of the brands which offer the same mouthpieces with a range of different backbores.

WEIGHT

All kinds of benefits are attributed to extra weight in a mouthpiece. That's why several brands sell mouthpieces in two versions: an 'ordinary' one and a weighted version which costs a little more. Weighted mouthpieces often have special names such as Mega Tone or Heavytop.

A more solid tone

The extra weight in a mouthpiece may help you produce a more 'solid' tone, to avoid distortion at high volumes and to achieve better control, both in general and over high notes. But as ever there are counter-arguments: many players find a non-weighted mouthpiece more responsive and better for controlling and colouring the tone, and others claim the difference is negligible.

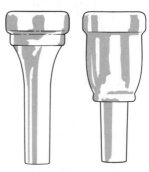

An ordinary cornet mouthpiece (short model) and a weighted version

Boosters

Rather than buying a weighted mouthpiece, you could opt for a *mouthpiece booster*. Some of these boosters resemble big, separate cups which you push onto the mouthpiece, while other designs are more like thick metal rings.

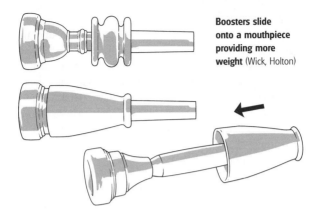

Boosters slide onto a mouthpiece providing more weight (Wick, Holton)

MATERIALS

Most mouthpieces are made of silver-plated brass, but of course there are other materials to choose from.

Silver or gold

Brass leaves an unpleasant taste and can cause a rash, so silver coating is no luxury. If your skin or your lips can't cope with silver either, a gold-plated mouthpiece may be the solution. However, they cost around £70/$100 or more, and gold plating doesn't last as long as silver plating.

Silver, aluminium, plastic and wood

Rather than a weighted, silver-plated mouthpiece, you could go for a solid silver one, which with its extra weight will give you a stronger, darker sound. At the opposite end of the scale are ultra-light aluminium mouthpieces which respond very easily and offer very bright high notes. For players who are allergic to all metals there are synthetic mouthpieces, or metal mouthpieces with a plastic rim. Wooden mouthpieces, which are even more rare, give a very soft, mellow tone.

AND FINALLY

You'll need to get used to a new mouthpiece, just as you would to a new pair of shoes. If you go straight ahead and play for hours with a new mouthpiece, you risk sore lips. And it can take a long time before you realize that your mouthpiece is causing problems.

Fifty mouthpieces or just one?

There are professional players who are still using the mouthpiece their teacher gave them thirty years ago. There are others who have tried at least fifty different mouthpieces and are still looking for the perfect one, which they may well never find. It's likely that a player who fits into the first category will have an 'easier' embouchure than a player of the second type, but some people just like experimenting. Thanks to the latter group, there are plenty of second-hand mouthpieces for sale.

Brands

Vincent Bach, Schilke and Yamaha are three well-known mouthpiece manufacturers that also make instruments. Other instrument brands like Courtois, Holton, Jupiter and Selmer also have their own mouthpieces, although they don't necessarily design or make them themselves. There are also brands which only supply mouthpieces, or only mouthpieces and accessories such as mutes. Greg Black, Giardinelli, Josef Klier, Jet-Tone, MMP (Marcinkiewicz), Bob Reeves, Stork and Denis Wick are some well-known examples.

7. MUTES

The only mutes that really mute your sound, so much so that it is muffled almost completely, are the practice mutes discussed in Chapter 3. Other types, rather than simply making your instrument quieter, are for creating particular effects, such as tone-colours that range from razor-sharp to velvety-soft.

Most types of mutes are hollow cones, which are held in place in the bell by a few strips or a ring of cork. The three best-known types of mute are the *straight mute*, the *cup mute* and the *harmon mute*, which is also known by a host of different names. The exact effect of each of these types, of course, varies between brands.

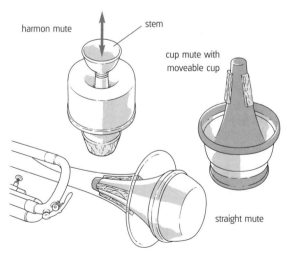

The three best-known mutes

Straight mute

The straight mute is the most commonly used type. If a classical piece specifies *con sordino* (with a mute) in a brass part, the player will almost always use a straight mute. It largely closes off the bell, making your instrument sound a little like someone talking whilst holding their nose – a touch nasal and a bit thin or shrill.

Cup mute

The cup mute looks like a straight mute with a cap. The inside of the cap is sometimes finished with thin, soft material, giving a softer, muffled sound. On some cup mutes, the cap is adjustable. The closer it is to the bell, the more it mutes the sound and the 'smaller' the sound becomes. Some cup mutes, with caps that can be moved right up against the bell, can double as practice mutes.

Harmon, wah-wah, wow, bubble...

The harmon mute has lots of different names, depending on the brand, from the *wow*, *wow-wow*, *wah-wah* and *bubble mute*, to *extending tube* and *E.T. mute*. This type of mute has a cork ring which closes off the bell entirely, the sound coming out of a hole in the mute only. As with the straight mute, the effect can be described as 'nasal' but it is slightly different nevertheless – a little more metallic, you could say. You can hear the effect on many recordings by the jazz trumpeter Miles Davis among others.

Laurel & Hardy

Harmon mutes virtually always come with a small adjustable pipe which you can stick into the hole. By opening and closing the hole of this *stem* with your hand you get the 'wow-wow' trumpet noises often used in Laurel & Hardy films.

Aluminium, wood and plastic

Most mutes are made of aluminium, which produces a brighter sound than wood or fibreglass. Some aluminium mutes have copper or brass bottoms (*ends*) making the sound more powerful and full. Plastic mutes, which sound softer than metal and brighter than wood, are generally cheaper to buy and more resilient to everything from knocks to rainwater. You may occasionally see mutes made entirely of steel, copper or another metal; these weigh and cost more.

Prices

Straight mutes cost anything from around £10/$15 to around £45/$60. The cheapest ones are usually made of fibreglass or plastic, whilst the most expensive are special aluminium mutes, with a copper bottom, for example. Harmon mutes are generally about twice the price of straight mutes, and cup mutes are somewhere in between. Trombone mutes cost more because they're bigger (usually around 50% more than the equivalent trumpet mutes).

Plunger

It's clear where the *plunger* mute gets its name from. If you find a sink plunger that fits your bell, you have a cheap solution. This type of mute is used for *doo-wah* effects: at the 'doo' you smother the sound by closing the bell, and at the 'wah' you take the mute off again. Some bands use hats, known as *Derby mutes*, instead of rubber or metal plungers. Prices for these start at around £35/$30.

A plunger

Bucket mute

A *bucket mute* or *velvet mute* is a small cylinder which attaches to the edge of the bell with small clamps. The mute is filled with a soft material such as mineral wool or foam plastic, making the instrument sound very soft, smooth and velvety. If you want to create a flugelhorn-like sound on a trumpet, a bucket mute is a good idea. Several brands produce these mutes in various depths – the deeper the mute, the greater the effect and the quieter the sound.

Other types

There are also various other types of mutes, such as textile mutes which fit over your bell, or even over another mute,

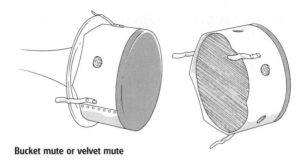

Bucket mute or velvet mute

and are held in place by a rubber band. Or *clear-tone mutes*, which look like two straight mutes fitted together. Certain other types come with names that describe the effect, from the sweetish *mel-o-wah* to the buzzing *wee-zee*, the penetrating *megaphone* and the whispering *whispa-mute*.

MORE ON MUTES

A mute not only makes your instrument sound different, it also makes it play differently. You have to work harder, your volume goes down and the pitch often goes up a little – especially the lower notes. If a note gets sharp because of the mute, just pull your tuning slide out a little. The amount you need to fine-tune, and how much harder you'll have to work, depend both on the type and the brand; badly designed mutes can make playing in tune very hard.

Moisten the cork

If you have a mute that won't stay in place properly, try moistening the cork strip(s) with a little water. If that doesn't work, the cork may need to be adjusted or replaced. Never force a mute into place.

Mute holders

You can get special mute holders, which can be attached to music stands. They are useful if you keep swapping between using a mute and not using it.

Brands

A few large, well-known manufacturers of mutes are Tom Crown, Humes & Berg, Jo-Ral and Denis Wick, and a few smaller ones are Charles Davis, Harmon, Spivak and the Swedish Ullvén brand.

8. BEFORE AND AFTER

Before you start playing, you need to make sure that your valves or slide are properly lubricated, and that your instrument is in tune. And taking a little care of your instrument when you've finished playing can save you a lot of cleaning time later. This chapter is full of tips on everything you should do before and after playing, plus tips on cases and gig bags, and on amplifying your instrument.

If you really want to keep your instrument in good condition, you'll need to do some work on it at home, too, such as rinsing and lubricating. You can read all about that in Chapter 9.

Out of the case, mouthpiece in

It's best to lift a trumpet, cornet or flugelhorn out of its case by the valve casings, and put the mouthpiece into the leadpipe with a light, twisting motion. Don't push or knock it in, or before you know it you'll need a mouthpiece puller to get it out.

Trombones

Always hold the bell section of a trombone by the bell stay, and when handling the slide always take hold of the inner and outer braces at the same time – even if you are certain that the slide lock is on. Hold the slide with the bow downwards and fit the bell into it with the other hand.

Perpendicular

Make sure the bell is perpendicular (90°) to the slide, and only then tighten the bell lock nut. Check again that you

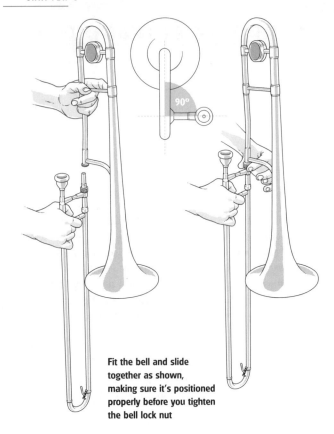

Fit the bell and slide
together as shown,
making sure it's positioned
properly before you tighten
the bell lock nut

still have a right angle before you tighten it fully. If you
twist the bell into place after you have tightened the nut,
you may not be able to get it loose again, as you can easily
apply more force by twisting the bell than you think. Only
fit the mouthpiece once you have assembled the trombone.

VALVES AND SLIDES

Valves must always be lubricated using special valve oil. In
order to do the job properly, as you should do regularly,
you need to take the valves right out (see Chapter 9).
However, that takes a while, so you can't do it before every
practice or performance – here are some quick tips.

Piston valves

If a valve gets a little slow, this probably means it's too long
since you oiled it. A quick solution is to hold your instru-

ment upside down and drip a little valve oil into the holes of the bottom cap whilst moving the valve up and down. Don't use too much oil, otherwise it will run straight out again.

Trombone slides

Lubricating a trombone slide is best done in advance – turn to page 93 to read how. Just before playing, all you need to do to help it move smoothly is sprinkle some cool tap water over the inner slide. A spray bottle is useful, and won't cost you much, and there are all kinds of special agents that can be added to the water. Some trombonists are convinced they help, though many prefer to do without. Make sure you always either empty the spray bottle or attach a tight lid to it before putting it in your case.

TUNING

Tuning your instrument is a very simple process: you move the tuning slide in or out until you get the correct pitch. The hard part is learning to hear when the pitch is exactly right. Producing the correct note, and holding it steady, can also take some practice.

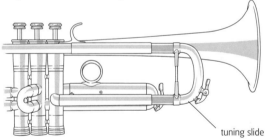

tuning slide

The extended tuning slide of a trumpet ...

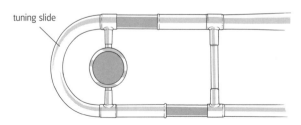

tuning slide

... and of a trombone

Temperature and tuning

If your instrument is very cold it may sound too low, so you'll need to warm it up before tuning. You can either breathe soundlessly through the instrument or play as normal to warm it up. Also, many players hold their mouthpiece in their hand or put it in a pocket before playing, as a cold mouthpiece feels quite uncomfortable. Never put a mouthpiece in a pocket with coins in it, as the rim may get scratched.

The 440 hertz A

Many orchestras and bands tune to the note A which is just to the right of the middle of a piano keyboard (see page 15). If you play this A on a piano, the strings vibrate 440 times per second – or, in technical terms, 440 hertz or 440 Hz. This is the same note produced by most tuning forks, which are thick metal forks that you tap against your knee and then hold next to your ear to hear the note. Many electronic metronomes can also produce this note.

A tuning fork

Second valve, second position

On a trumpet, a flugelhorn or a cornet you get a concert pitch A by playing a B (pressing the second valve). On a trombone you play the A with the slide in the second position. If you have an instrument with an F-attachment, the attachment needs to be tuned separately.

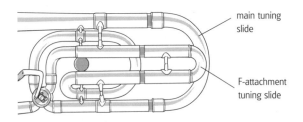

main tuning slide

F-attachment tuning slide

The F-attachment needs to be tuned separately

Tuning to B flat

Brass bands and concert bands usually tune to the note B flat, in which case you play a C (without valves) on a trumpet, cornet or flugelhorn. On a trombone, you play the B flat in the closed position.

How far?

When you're starting out, tuning can be tricky. You have to learn to hear when you are properly in tune. Besides, when you're a beginner it isn't easy to play the A or B flat in exactly the same way each time. Generally, you shouldn't have to extend the tuning slide more than an inch (2.5cm) and fine-tuning is often a matter of less than a tenth of an inch (under half a millimetre).

In and out

In the beginning, you may have trouble hearing any difference when you move the tuning slide. If so, try extending it as far as it will go, and play a note. Then push it back all the way in, and play the same note: then you'll find it easier to hear what 'too high' (sharp) and 'too low' (flat) sound like.

Tuners

You can also use an electronic tuner. These devices show you whether your instrument is tuned too high, too low or exactly right. And, on a well-tuned instrument, you can use a tuner to see if you are playing any particular note in tune. Most tuners have a small microphone built-in, but you can also get tuners that clamp onto an instrument and 'feel' the pitch. This type responds only to what you play – it doesn't also pick up notes from someone sitting next to you.

New mouthpiece?

When using a different mouthpiece you may find that you need to extend the tuning slide further or less far. This may be because the new mouthpiece fits further or less far into the receiver, or because the bore, cup or backbore are different.

Weak

If you need to extend the tuning slide almost fully, for instance because you are tuning to a piano which is itself tuned too low, you won't just get a lower note. You'll also hear that the sound is different, and that the intonation be-comes worse, with certain notes deviating more than usual.

A little higher

Some orchestras tune just a little higher than most – for instance to a 442 hertz A. There are tuning forks which produce that pitch too, and many electronic tuners can be adjusted to different pitches.

AFTER

It's easiest to keep a mouthpiece clean by simply rinsing it under a tap after playing. If your case or gig bag doesn't have a mouthpiece holder, keep it in a leather or synthetic pouch – you should be able to pick one up for less than £5/$8. You should always put a mouthpiece down on its side to avoid scratches and dents to the rim, but never put it in a position where it may roll off a table or other surface.

Removing moisture

When you play, you'll frequently have to remove the mois-ture that collects in your instrument by blowing through it while opening the water key. When you've finished play-ing, the best way to remove most of the moisture is to re-move the valve slides, and then blow through the instru-ment. A tip: when pulling out a valve slide, always press down the corresponding valve.

The dryer the better

The better you dry the parts of your instrument, the longer they will stay clean and the longer they will last. Some players leave their cases ajar after they've finished playing, so that everything can continue drying.

The tuning slide

After playing, it's best to push your tuning slide completely in. This way there will be less chance of it eventually getting stuck.

Clean teeth

To keep their instruments as clean as possible, many players brush or even floss their teeth before playing. This way less stuff gets into your mouthpiece and the instrument itself.

Cloth

Sweat can damage lacquer, brass and even silver. So run a soft, clean, lint-free cloth over your instrument after playing, not forgetting the inside of the bell. An old T-shirt (unprinted) or a dishcloth will do fine.

Cases

New instruments usually come with a rectangular case with one or more holes for mouthpieces and a separate compartment for a bottle of valve oil and other small bits and pieces. Trombone cases almost always flare out slightly at the bell. If you want an alternative to a straightforward case, there are all kinds you can choose from.

More space

Most standard rectangular cases can take a knock and often have the most extra space. The larger models have room for accessories like one or more mutes, a music stand and sheet music, and there are even cases which hold two instruments. Basic cases start at around £35/$50, while the most luxurious models cost at least five times as much. Trombone cases are, as you'd expect, more expensive. Check whether a trombone case has 'feet' on the long side, the end where the bell goes or both.

Gig bags

Gig bags are padded bags made of canvas, synthetic material or leather. Most are quite small, though they usually have one or more extra compartments and come with

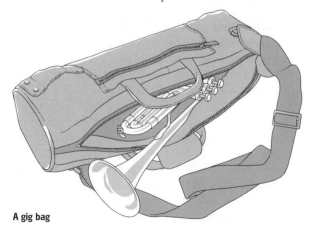

A gig bag

shoulder straps. There are also larger gig bags that hold two instruments (such as a trumpet and cornet) as well as a stand, mutes and music. You can buy a decent gig bag for around £35/$50 but prices go up to around £150/$200 for special designs or materials. Most gig bags won't protect your instrument against knocks as well as a case does, but they are easier to carry around. And if you don't want everyone to know that you have an instrument with you, you can get a gig bag that looks pretty much like a normal shoulder bag – unless you happen to play the trombone.

Shaped cases
There are also shaped or contoured cases, made of a hard synthetic material in the shape of the instrument. They're smaller than rectangular cases, which means they hold less, but some are just as strong.

Locks
Most cases can be locked. More than anything, the small locks are there to prevent the lid springing open if the case falls. They are unlikely to stop anyone stealing the instrument.

Locks and hinges
When choosing a case or gig bag, check to see how sturdy the locks, zips, hinges, handgrips and carrying straps are – this is generally a good test of quality. Clips and rings made of plastic are not usually as strong as metal ones.

STANDS AND MICROPHONES
It's handy to have a stand for your instrument for when you're taking a short break from playing. And if you often have to play at loud volumes, with a jazz or Latin band, for example, a suitable microphone can prove useful.

Stands
Most trumpet stands are simple tripods with a cone that the bell fits onto. The smallest ones are designed to fold up and fit inside the bell, and therefore the instrument's case, for storage. For a flugelhorn, of course, you need one with an extra-large cone, and trombone stands are much bigger still – about the size of a sturdy music stand when folded

up. Stands vary greatly with respect to sturdiness and how easy they are to fold up.

A mini stand for trumpet or cornet, which folds up and fits inside the bell for storage

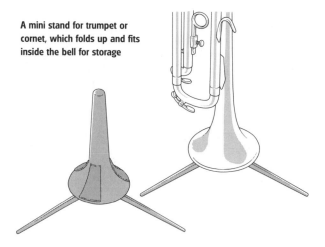

No stand?

A tip for if you don't have a stand: always lay a trumpet or a cornet on its left side, because the second valve slide makes the right side much more prone to damage.

Microphones

Most good vocal microphones also work well for brass instruments. But using a traditional microphone on a stand has one disadvantage: you have to constantly aim your bell directly at it. One solution is to use a special clip-on microphone that attaches to your instrument, and if you really like the freedom to move around you could buy one with a cordless systems, though these are very expensive.

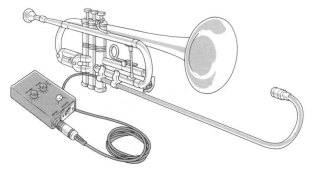

Trumpet microphone with clamp and pre-amplifier (SD Systems)

Prices for clip-on microphones are around £100–350/ $150–500.

Pre-amps
Many clip-on microphones require a small pre-amplifier, or pre-amp, which boosts the signal before sending it to the main amplifier. The pre-amp (like the transmitter for a cordless system) usually clips onto your belt.

Amplifiers and effects
Brass players generally use far fewer electronic effects than electric guitarists, but the use of reverb and delay is quite common, and flanger, chorus and wah-wah can be fun to experiment with. A keyboard amplifier works well for general use.

SAFETY TIPS
An instrument can be a serious investment. Here are a few extra tips on keeping yours safe.

Insurance
Depending on their value, musical instruments usually fall into the category of 'valuables' for home insurance. This means you have to let your insurance company know you have an instrument in order for it to be covered. Some home insurance policies also allow you to take out extra cover for your instrument to protect it when you take it out of the house. This can be quite expensive, but it means the instrument will be covered against theft and damage, whether you're on the road, at a practice or on stage. Some insurance companies also do specific policies for musicians.

Serial number
Note down the serial number of your instrument, as it may be required by your insurance company or the police if the instrument is ever stolen or lost. There's a form to do this on pages 128–129. You'll usually find the serial number under the thumb hook, on or near the bell or on the valve casings.

Storing your instrument
Always store your instrument in its case or bag, rather than

leaving it on a table or a chair. And never leave an instrument where it can get too hot – high temperatures can cause valves and valve slides to jam. Brass gets hotter than you might think in the sun.

Rucksacks

If you are transporting an instrument with the case in an upright position, in a rucksack for example, always pack the case so the bell is pointing upwards.

9. MAINTENANCE

Your instrument will sound and look better for longer, and hold its value better, if you clean it regularly. And valves and slides need oiling or greasing from time to time. This chapter provides tips on jobs you can do yourself, and suggests what you should leave to a professional.

Keeping the outside of your instrument clean is very simple. There are all kinds of cloths and even polishing gloves which not only clean but also shine your instrument and sometimes even add a thin layer which protects against sweat and dirt. Of course, an ordinary cloth with a little special instrument cleaner will do the job too.

Lacquer and silver

There are different cloths, gloves and cleaners on sale for lacquered and silver-plated instruments, and there are only a few which you can use for both. Using the wrong one may damage your lacquer or silver plate. Ordinary silver or brass polish is cheaper than the types sold in music shops, but it isn't the same stuff. It's too abrasive, and can leave scratches and remove the lacquer finish.

Silver plating

Silver polishing cloths get very black after a certain amount of use. Contrary to what you might think, the blacker they get, the better they work. Never wash a silver polishing cloth, as this turns it into an ordinary piece of cloth. Silver-plated instruments should be polished very rarely in order to avoid wearing down the extremely thin plating.

Covers

If you find dull patches on your instrument on and around the valves, you may have quite acidic sweat. The solution is to buy a slip-on *valve cover* or *handguard*. Genuine leather valve covers are more expensive than synthetic ones but feel more comfortable. When you are polishing, don't forget to

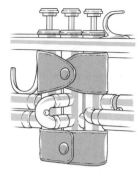

Valve cover

polish under the cover, and clean the cover itself now and then. Similar handguards are available for trombonists.

Other techniques

Many players have different methods of protecting the vulnerable parts of their instruments, such as winding a length of gaffer tape or duct tape around them. This won't look or feel as good as leather and you may have trouble getting the tape off again, but it will save you some money.

VALVES, SLIDES AND VALVE SLIDES

A valve slide shouldn't move as easily as a valve piston, and piston valves need a thinner type of oil than rotary valves. Some perfectionists use six or seven different bottles of oil or grease 0on their instrument whilst others make do with just two – but this is the minimum. Most of these products cost around £3/$5.

Valve oil

To keep piston valves moving smoothly you need valve oil – a lubricant that is almost as runny as water. Some brands are as odourless as water too. How often you need to oil your valves depends on your instrument and on how often you play. But when the valves stop moving smoothly, you've left it a little too long. For tips on quick lubrication during a rehearsal or performance, see page 78.

Removing the pistons

If you want to do a proper oiling job, remove the pistons from their valve casings one by one. Be careful, because they're hollow, and the thin walls are easily dented. First wipe the piston clean with a lint-free cloth, apply about three or four drops of oil to it and replace it with a light, twisting motion. This way the oil will spread around the whole piston and the inside of the valve casing, and you can feel the piston guides slot into place. On some instruments you can also see whether the valves are in the right positions in their casings.

Replacing the pistons

If a valve is in the wrong position, the instrument will make 'Donald Duck' type noises or no sound at all, as it will if replaced in the wrong casing. A tip: replace the oiled valve and play briefly to check that it's properly in place. Only then tighten the valve cap and take out the next valve. Valve caps will stay in place if you turn them finger-tight – don't use any force, let alone a wrench.

All three

If you do remove all three valves at once, remember which goes where. If they have numbers on them, valve 1 always goes closest to the mouthpiece.

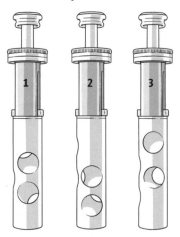

Some valves have numbers

Thicker oil

If you find standard valve oil too runny, try to get a thicker type – never try Vaseline or an equivalent as an alternative as it may make your valves stick.

The second valve

Eventually the valve felts start to wear. If they become too thin, the pistons will go down too far, preventing a smooth airflow and making you blow too hard. To check the felts, remove the second valve slide, press in the second valve and look inside. If you see that the ports are going down too far, so that they are no longer directly in line with the tubes of the valve slides, the felts need replacing.

The leadpipe

Letting a few drops of valve oil trickle into the mouthpiece receiver and leadpipe is a good way to protect the tubing against the acids in your saliva, which can corrode the metal. Give the screw threads of the valve caps a tiny drop, too, to prevent them from sticking.

Rotary valves

Rotary valves need slightly thicker oil, usually named *rotor oil* or *rotary oil*. These valves can be lubricated from the outside. Most of them require you to unscrew a cap on one side and a screw on the other before you apply the oil, but you don't need to dismantle the entire valve.

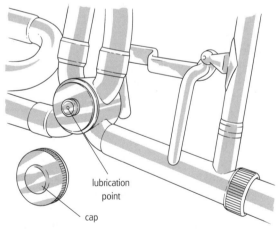

lubrication
point

cap

A lubrication point on the rotor of a trombone F-attachment

Through the tube

You can also lubricate rotors by removing the slide and letting a few drops of oil fall inside the tubing which leads to the rotor.

Distribute the oil

To distribute the oil evenly, operate the rotor a few times and turn the whole instrument (only the bell section for a trombone) around a few times. There is a special type of oil available for the hinges of the lever.

String actions

If you have an F-attachment with a string action, check occasionally to make sure the string is not about to break, and carry in your case a spare piece of string, a screwdriver to fasten it and a drawing of how to fit it. Without the latter, fitting a string is surprisingly difficult. Check if there's a diagram in your instrument's manual – the example shown on the left may not be right for your F-attachment.

How to fit a string to an F-attachment

Valve slides

Valve slides, on trumpets, cornets and flugelhorns, should not slide as easily as pistons, so *slide oil* or *slide grease* is less runny than valve oil. It may be preferable for the adjustable (third and first) valve slides to move a little more easily than the tuning slide or the second valve slide. For this reason some brands produce thinner (*light*) grease and a slightly thicker type – some even produce special tuning slide grease.

Using one type

A good alternative to using loads of different greases is to use the same slide grease for all the slides, and apply a drop of valve oil to the first and third valve slides if they are a little too stiff. A tuning slide that moves of its own accord needs slightly thicker grease. If the bow is removable, then lubricate it occasionally; otherwise it may become very difficult to remove.

Vaseline

Some money-conscious players use non-acidic Vaseline for their slides. Vaseline is cheaper than special grease, but a small pot of slide grease will last you ages, it's less sensitive to cold and heat and it does exactly what it's made for.

Applying the grease

Remove the slide you want to lubricate from your instrument, clean it with a cloth and dab a small amount of grease on both ends. Wipe away the excess grease so that it doesn't end up in the tubes. Slide one of the ends into its tube and twist it round a couple of times: this will ensure the grease is well distributed. Take it off, and do the same with the other end, then replace the slide. Usually there's only one way you can put the slide back, and if you try to replace it putting the wrong end in the wrong tube, the slide won't go in – not all the way at least.

Trombone slides

The trombone slide is like one huge valve slide, but because it needs to slide a good deal more easily it requires a different lubricant. *Trombone slide cream* or *slide oil* is widely used. New slides need to be lubricated daily, but once the instrument is 'played in' you may not need to do it so often.

Skin cream

Trombonists, like other brass players, experiment with alternative solutions. Some swear by certain types of furniture polish or skin cream instead of dedicated slide cream. Again, when you consider how long it lasts, special trombone cream isn't really all that expensive – and you can be confident it will work well and not damage your instrument.

Handling the slide

The metal of the inner slide is only around a hundredth of an inch (0.25mm) thick, so it dents and bends easily. When lubricating your slide, dismantle it carefully and lay the outer slide in your case. Wipe the tubes clean one by one, always towards the ends. Never hold the instrument by one of the tubes, and avoid touching one whilst you are cleaning or lubricating the other.

Turning

Next, spread a little cream around the first tube and wipe off the excess. Stick the tube into the outer slide and turn it around a few times. Do the same with the second tube. If you are going to play straight away, spray on a little water to make the slide action extra-smooth (see page 79).

Only part of the tubes

Some trombonists prefer to grease only the first part of each tube. Then they move the slide in and out a few times, and spray it afterwards. That way there's less chance of dented and bent tubes, and the cream will spread around the slide anyway as you play.

Other parts

Dab a little grease on the bell lock nut now and again, as well as on the shank of your mouthpiece and the slide lock. This way you'll avoid anything getting stuck.

INSIDE

To keep your instrument in the best possible condition, you need to clean the inside every two or three months. You should clean your mouthpiece, mouthpiece receiver and leadpipe more often, as they are the first parts to get clogged up by whatever you blow into the instrument.

The mouthpiece

If you don't clean your mouthpiece now and then, the bore will gradually get smaller and smaller. Rinsing it under the tap after every session is a good start. About once a week, clean the mouthpiece a bit more thoroughly with a little washing-up liquid and a special mouthpiece brush. Keep pulling the brush through the mouthpiece until it comes out clean.

Bowls and pans

To remove lime-scale from your mouthpiece, put it in a bowl of water with a large dash of cleaning vinegar, or leave it to soak for a few hours in some water with washing-up liquid or washing soda in it. Some players even dissolve some washing soda in a pan of water and boil their mouthpiece. If you try this, be sure to rinse your mouthpiece with lots of cold water before touching it (brass doesn't cool quickly) and make sure the rim doesn't get scratched in the pan.

In the bath

To clean the inside of your instrument, it's handy if you use a bath. Run enough lukewarm water to submerge your instrument completely. Add some green soap, or possibly some mild shampoo, but not washing-up liquid, washing soda, vinegar or other cleaning agents. Lay a towel on the bottom of the bath, to prevent scratches, and lay your instrument on top of it. A trombone should always be bathed in three sections, ideally one at a time: the bell, the inner slide and the outer slide. If you have an instrument with piston valves, take the pistons out; rotary valves can stay in place.

Tub or waste bin

If you don't have a bath, a plastic washing-up bowl, a clean waste bin or a baby's bathtub may be just big enough. Failing that, allow some lukewarm water to run through each tube for a little while. This is also a good method if you only want to clean the leadpipe.

Not too hot

Don't run the water too hot. You may burn yourself touching the instrument, and the heat is likely to damage a lacquer finish.

Cleaners, snakes and brushes

You can clean the insides of the wet tubes using a *bore cleaner* or *s*, a flexible coiled spring with brushes at either end. You can also buy special valve brushes, though the valve casings, and the portholes in the pistons, can be cleaned by simply pulling a clean handkerchief through them.

A bore cleaner, a valve brush and a mouthpiece brush

Spit balls

An alternative way to clean the inside of your instrument is to use *spit balls* or *s*pit corks, which you blow through the

95

tubing. These shouldn't be used for instruments with a very small bore or tight bends in the tubing, such as a piccolo trumpet.

Drying and greasing

Rinse all the tubes with clean soap-free water once they are clean. Carefully shake the instrument (or section of the instrument), blow out as much water as you can, dry the outside and leave everything until it is dry on the inside too. Then grease the valves and the slide(s), put some grease on the shank of your mouthpiece, spray a drop of oil into the leadpipe and oil the hinges of the water keys while you're at it. Amado water keys can always use a drop of oil, too.

Scale and tarnish

To remove scale and tarnish from the inside of the instrument, you'll need to get it thoroughly cleaned by a professional.

Maintenance sets

Many brands sell complete maintenance sets containing various brushes, a cleaning cloth, oil and grease, and sometimes even spare felts for valves or corks for water keys.

PROBLEMS

If your instrument is dented, if a soldered seam has come loose, or if your mouthpiece, a valve, a slide or anything else is stuck, the best advice is to take it to a professional. Bending, soldering or using wrenches or other tools on your instrument is always risky, not least because brass instruments are made of very thin metal.

A stuck mouthpiece

You can sometimes get a stuck mouthpiece loose by holding it under the cold tap for a while. Wrapping a cloth around it may give you better grip, but if you can't get it out that way, take the instrument to a professional – never try using pliers or a vice to get a mouthpiece free. If the instrument won't fit into its case because of the stuck mouthpiece, wrap it in a large towel for the time being.

Cloth

If a valve slide is jammed, push a cloth through the bow and pull out the valve slide with the cloth. Be careful, so it doesn't suddenly come free and damage anything. If you think you need to pull too hard, take it to a professional.

Overhaul

A proper overhaul is a job for a professional too. This includes replacing felts, springs and corks, smoothing out dents, polishing and regulating. Also the instrument will get a special bath to dissolve chalk scale and oxidation. The whole job usually costs roughly £70–150/$100–200. The bigger and dirtier the instrument is, the higher the price will be. Most instruments won't need an overhaul more than once every five years.

10. BACK IN TIME

The trombone hasn't changed much over the last four centuries and even the valved trumpet is nearly 200 years old. You have to go back thousands of years to meet the earliest ancestors of these instruments.

Wind instruments made of shells, hollowed-out pieces of wood and animal horns have been around for millennia – the double meaning of the word 'horn' is no coincidence.

A horn made of horn, with holes for playing different notes

Bronze

Only much later did the first metal instruments appear. They were often made of bronze, gold or silver and were originally no more than a long straight tube, a bit wider at one end, with the other end flattened slightly for the lips.

Around the world

Over the millennia, trumpet-like instruments have developed in many parts of the world. From the Greek *salpinx*, the bronze Celtic *carnyx* and the Roman *lituus*, over two thousand years ago, to the medieval European *buisine* and the fifteen-foot long, copper Tibetan *dung*. And these are just a few examples.

Bends

Only just over six hundred years ago did craftsmen learn how to bend tubes without getting kinks in them, and the trumpet gradually began to look a little bit like the present-day instrument. In those days it was mainly used as a signal instrument, with the player able to produce only seven or eight different notes (the harmonic series).

A signal trumpet without valves

Slide trumpets

Not much later, the *slide trumpet* developed, which allowed the trumpeter to play many more notes. It was an awkward thing to play, though – on some you had to slide the entire instrument backwards and forwards. The trombone (Italian for large trumpet) came a little later, and was a much better solution. Originally called the *sackbut*, the trombone has looked very similar for a long time – examples from more than four centuries ago look remarkably like modern-day instruments.

The first valves

In the eighteenth century, an anonymous instrument-maker devised a system of keys for the trumpet, but it wasn't ideal. The breakthrough came in 1815, when the

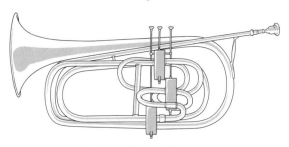

The earliest valves looked a bit like matchboxes

German craftsmen Blühmel and Stölzel created the first real valve, which looked something like a metal matchbox. In 1839 the Frenchman Périnet added a few improvements, and since then this type of valve has been known as a Périnet valve. A few years earlier, the Austrian trumpet-maker Riedl had invented the rotary valve.

The flugelhorn...

Originally, the flugelhorn was a small metal horn played by the horsemen who rode on the far left and right flanks (*Flügel*, in German) of a hunting party. Long ago, some flugelhorns were made with keys, like those on a saxophone, and in around 1850 the first flugelhorns with valves appeared. The modern instrument evolved from there, with numerous instrument-makers improving and varying the design. The original valveless flugelhorn, which is still used, is commonly referred to as the *bugle*.

...and the cornet

The cornet, which means 'little horn', was invented in France at the beginning of the nineteenth century, when valves were added to a small French or German horn. Within a few decades it became the chief treble instrument in British brass bands and American wind and military bands, for which the brighter-sounding American version of the instrument was developed.

11. THE FAMILY

Essentially, all brass instruments are very similar – they only really vary in the length of their tubing, how conical it is, and whether they have valves or a slide. This chapter introduces some more members of the brass family.

Many brass instruments come in various keys, such as the C trumpet and the E flat cornet mentioned in Chapter 2. Trumpets especially come in lots of different keys.

Piccolo to bass

A little smaller than a C trumpet is the *soprano trumpet* in D, E flat or E. Another size smaller and higher is the *sopranino*, and the very smallest, highest-sounding model is the *piccolo trumpet* or *Bach trumpet*, in A and B flat. There are also lower-sounding trumpets, such as the F trumpet and the bass trumpet in B flat.

Two tunings

Smaller trumpets can often be played in two keys, and some even in three. If you buy a G/F trumpet, for instance, it will probably come with two leadpipes, a set of extra valve slides and an extra tuning slide, or even a second bell. When you are playing in F you use the longer tubes and valve slides, and if you need a G trumpet you use the shorter ones. There are also flugelhorns that can play in C, D and E flat. The more extra parts you get with a two-key instrument, the better the intonation can be in both keys.

Four valves

Piccolo trumpets often have four valves, and there are also

flugelhorns with four. The fourth valve lowers the note by a fourth (from F to C, for instance), just like an F-attachment on a trombone.

Pocket-sized

The *pocket trumpet* looks smaller than it really is: if you were to roll it out, it'd be just as long as a regular B flat trumpet, and it sounds the same pitch, too. Pocket-sized cornets are also available.

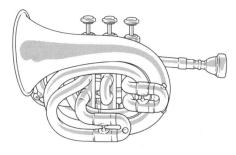

A pocket trumpet is actually the same length as a normal trumpet

Variations

There are many more trumpet variations, such as jazz trumpeter Dizzy Gillespie's instrument with a tilted bell, and instruments with two bells. There are also massively long instruments like the Herald or Triumphal trumpets, or the equally stretched *Aida trumpet,* designed for use in Verdi's 1871 opera.

Trombones

As well as the tenor, alto and bass trombones, there are also *soprano* or *mini trombones* in B flat, plus the rare *contrabass trombone* and the *cimbasso,* the Italian contrabass.

Brass crossbreeds

Just about every brass instrument 'crossbreed' you could think of exists. The Holton Superbone has two piston valves, like a trum-

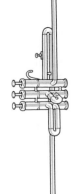

An Aida trumpet with three valves

pet, but it also has a slide, like a trombone. The Kanstul Flugelbone looks like a flugelhorn but sounds like a trombone. And then there's the *flumpet*, which is somewhere between a flugelhorn and a trumpet.

LOW BRASS

Low brass is a term used to describe low-pitched brass instruments such as the bass trombone, the tuba and the euphonium. These instruments are also known as *background brass*, as they're mainly used for accompaniments, and hardly ever for solos. They often have more valves, up to six, and all have a very conical tube.

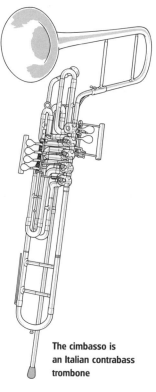

The cimbasso is an Italian contrabass trombone

Tuba

The name *tuba* usually refers to the bass tuba, which has a tube of around 25 feet. Bass tubas come in C, for symphony orchestras, and in B flat, for brass and concert bands. One size smaller are the tubas in F and E flat. In brass bands the word 'bass' is often used instead of tuba.

Euphonium

The *euphonium*, which is like a tenor tuba, is pitched one octave higher than the bass tuba in B flat.

Saxhorns

Around 1845, when Adolphe Sax was still perfecting his saxophone, he was granted a patent on a whole family of *saxhorns*. A few of these are still in use – the *tenor horn* and the *baritone* are most popular in brass bands. The baritone is very similar to the euphonium, but a euphonium has a wider bore and larger bell, and as a result sounds somewhat bigger and warmer. The two lowest-sounding saxhorns

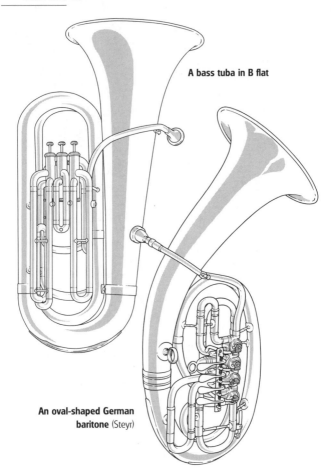

A bass tuba in B flat

An oval-shaped German baritone (Steyr)

are pretty much the same instruments as the large B flat and E flat tubas.

Different names

Many brass instruments have different names in different countries: a tenor horn is called alto or althorn in some, and a baritone in others. And often instruments with the same names look different in various countries. German saxhorns, for example, have an oval shape, though they sound no different.

French horn and mellophone

Brass instruments and saxes are often described as 'horns', but technically the word horn refers specifically to the

French horn, a very distinctive instrument used in orchestras and concert bands, though not generally in brass bands. You operate the rotary valves of a French horn with your left hand, and use your right hand like a mute, putting it in the bell to dampen the sound. The *mellophone* is a similar instrument that is used in marching bands (often played by French-horn players). It sounds a little bit brighter, and looks like a large, fat trumpet.

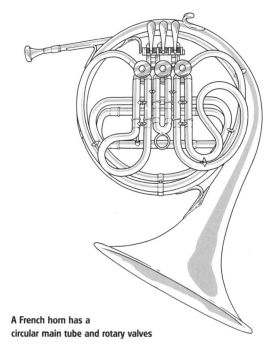

A French horn has a circular main tube and rotary valves

OTHER RELATIVES

Other members of the brass family include instruments specially designed for marching bands and various signal instruments.

Marching instruments

Large instruments like tubas are tricky to play if you're marching. The *sousaphone* solves this problem: it's a tuba in a circular form so that you can 'wear' it around your neck. It has an enormous forward-facing bell, which is often made of something lighter than brass, such as fibreglass.

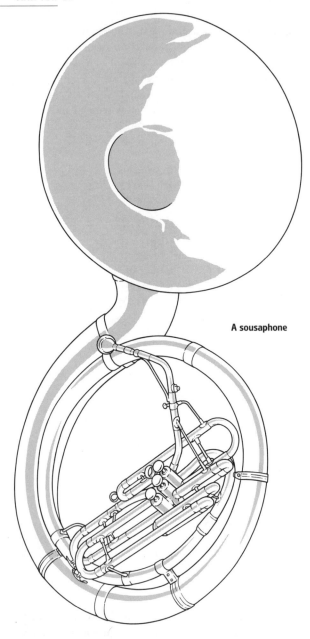

A sousaphone

On your shoulder

You can also get euphoniums, horns and tubas that are designed to rest on your shoulder to make them easier to march with. The bells of these instruments usually point forwards, instead of upwards, so the sound is projected towards the audience.

Without valves

An instrument without valves can only play harmonics – the notes of the harmonic series. Such instruments are called *natural instruments*. Two well- known examples are the *signal trumpet*, also called the *clarion*, and the *hunting horn*, but there are also valveless flugelhorns (bugles) and cornets. Natural instruments are primarily used in military and hunting contexts, though also in classical orchestras using 'period instruments'. These orchestras perform with the types of instruments that were in use when a piece of music was written. When Bach wrote his *Brandenburg Concerto No. 2*, for example, valves hadn't been invented. At a period instrument performance of the work, the player would use a valveless trumpet, which is now called a *baroque trumpet*, Bach trumpet or natural trumpet.

What about the sax?

Many people think of the saxophone as a brass instrument, because it has a brass tube with a flared bell at the end. However, instead of valves saxes have keys like a clarinet or a flute, and the sound is made using a reed. So, although it's made of brass, the sax belongs to the *woodwind* family (as does the flute, though it's almost always made of metal).

12. HOW THEY'RE MADE

Some companies still make their instruments almost entirely by hand, whilst others leave most of the work to computer-controlled machines. Here's a quick look at some of the various processes used in brass instrument manufacture.

Many expensive instruments have bells made of a single plate of brass. The plate is cut precisely to size, folded double and the seam soldered. To make the brass easier to hammer into shape later on, the metal is often rolled in a mill at this stage. The resulting shape resembles a squashed tulip.

Hammers

The bell-to-be is then placed on a die approximately the shape of the inside of the finished bell. Traditionally, wooden hammers are then used to shape the brass around the die. But in some factories, the bells are shaped by machines.

Two parts

In the case of a two-piece bell, the widest part (the actual bell-shaped section) is made separately. Usually, it is made from a brass disc which is rotated and pressed into shape, a process called *spinforming*. Altogether, this technique involves less work, so two-piece bells are cheaper than one-piece types.

A two-piece bell before assembly

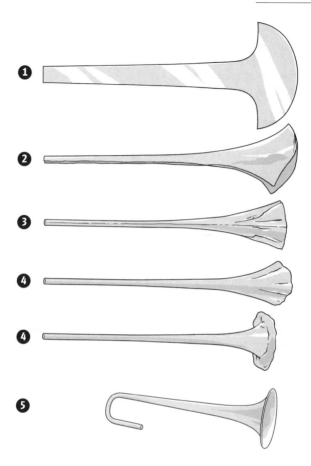

Making a one-piece bell
a flat sheet of brass (1), folded (2), soldered and rolled (3), roughly
hammered into shape (4), bent and finished (5)

The bends

To stop the tubes kinking when they are bent, they are first
filled. In the past they would use molten lead. Today it's
more likely to be sand or a kind of soapy mixture that's
frozen inside the tube. The tube is then bent, defrosted,
and emptied.

Bullets

Shorter tubes, like the second valve slide, are made perfectly round on the inside by forcing steel balls, or *bullets*,
through them.

Valves
Made in the traditional way, valves and pistons (one piston being made out of four tubes: the piston itself, and the three 'porthole tubes' that run through it) are assembled by hand, one at a time.

Tidying up
Before the instrument is finished, all the parts must be made to fit precisely: the tuning slide must fit the leadpipe, the valve slides must fit the valves and the pistons must fit the valve casings so they can move as smoothly as they should and without any leaks. All soldered seams have to be made invisible, and imperfect edges beaten smooth.

Assembly
Finally the instrument is buffed to a shine, lacquered or plated, assembled, checked and shipped.

Lathe
Mouthpieces are usually made on a lathe. The mouthpiece itself rotates and a special kind of chisel takes away the metal that has to be removed. Sometimes the chisel is guided by hand but usually a computer does this job.

13. THE BRANDS

There are thousands of manufacturers of trumpets, trombones, cornets and flugelhorns – from one-man workshops to large factories. This chapter provides an overview of some of the most important.

The following list looks at the larger, well-known factories, most of which produce all four of the instruments covered in this book, and in most price ranges. And some of them make instruments or parts for other brands too. Following that, a number of smaller and more exclusive brands are listed.

 The Czech Amati brand also makes saxes and flutes, and quite a few other brands have their instruments or certain components built for them by Amati. The brand Cerveny, part of the same house, mainly makes low brass instruments.

The factory of B&S (Blechblass & Signalinstrumente), in what used to be East Germany, produces just about all types of brass instruments. B&S also makes instruments for other brands, in all price ranges.

The Austrian trumpet player and engineer Vincent Bach made his first mouthpieces in 1918 after moving to America, and about six years later he built his first trumpet. The Bach company has long been one of the best-known brand names. It makes top-quality instruments, and also produces low-budget beginners' instruments under the name Elkhart.

The brands named after trumpet player Elden Benge, cornettist Charles Conn and trombonist Thomas King all belong to the American company United Musical Instruments (UMI). In Europe, Benge sells only trombones, and pocket and piccolo trumpets. Conn is best known for its Connstellation trumpet, and King for its trombones.

BESSON
LONDON

The Frenchman Gustave Auguste Besson made his first cornet in 1837. Twenty years later he moved to England. The series called French Besson is built in an American factory.

Antoine Courtois The French brand Courtois is also named after its founder: the small letter A, attached to the C-shaped little finger ring on many models, stands for Antoine, who made his first instrument in 1803.

T.J. Getzen, who was taught his trade by trombonist Frank Holton, opened a repair workshop in New York in 1939. A couple of years later he made his first trombones, and not much later he added trumpets and cornets to his range. Getzen also produces instruments for other brands, for instance Edwards, a brand established by Edward Getzen.

HOLTON◀
LebLanc◀
Martin◀

Frank Holton played the trombone in the band led by John Philip Sousa, after whom the sousaphone is named. Holton made his first instruments over a hundred years ago. Together with Martin, one of the few brands that produce coloured trumpets, the brand now belongs to the Leblanc company, which has been based in the US since 1950. Georges Leblanc had assumed control of the French company Noblet, itself founded in 1750, in 1904.

JUPITER SINCE 1930 ® Jupiter, one of the few large Taiwanese manufacturers, mainly offers instruments in the lower and middle price ranges. They make a well-known trombone designed especially for children.

KANSTUL MUSICAL INSTRUMENTS Zigmant Kanstul, founder of the fairly new American company Kanstul, learned his trade while working for various companies including Besson, King and the now defunct brand Olds. Kanstul also makes a lot of instruments for other brands.

YAMAHA The one-man Japanese organ factory started by Torakusu Yamaha in 1889 is now the world's largest manufacturer of musical instruments. Yamaha produces everything from drums to grand pianos, from bass guitars and amplifiers to piccolo trumpets and an extensive selection of mouthpieces – not to mention motorbikes, hi-fi equipment and bathtubs.

Other brands
Besides those listed, there are countless less well-known and smaller brands. A few examples: the only brass instruments made by the Taiwanese brand **BC Belcanto** are trumpets; **Blessing** and **Burbank** are a US brand found mainly in the lower and middle price ranges in Europe; and **Kühnl & Hoyer** is a German company.

Professional only
There are quite a few companies that only make professional-quality instruments. The German brand **Alexander**, best known for its horns, also makes an instrument that can be used as both a flugelhorn and a trumpet, thanks to interchangeable bells and leadpipes. The surname of Renold **Schilke** is only found on mouthpieces or on American-made trumpets and cornets costing around £2000/$3500 or more. Schilke is one of the few brands which sells instruments without mouthpieces. The Spanish **Stomvi** brand is best known for its combination mouthpieces. **Selmer**, based in France, is one of the world's largest producers of saxophones, but the company also builds professional trumpets and cornets. The Swiss firm **Willson**

makes flugelhorns plus trombones with its own Rotax valves. In Britain, Michael **Rath** specializes in handcrafted trombones, and handcrafted trumpets are available from **Taylor**, **Smith** and from **Wedgewood**.

More

There are many more high-quality brands, some of which are not available in all countries. A few examples are the American makes **Monette** and **Calicchio**, and the French brand **Couesnon**.

14. ORCHESTRAS AND BANDS

If you play trumpet, cornet, flugelhorn or trombone, there are all kinds of bands, orchestras and groups you can play in. In this chapter you'll read about which instruments are found in which ensembles, from symphony orchestras to funk bands.

The biggest type of classical orchestra, the symphony orchestra, can contain more than a hundred musicians. The violinists are the largest group, often numbering more than twenty. A large orchestra may have five trumpet players and three or four trombonists, along with French horn and tuba players, woodwind players, percussionists, harpists and a pianist. A chamber orchestra is smaller, usually having two trumpets and two trombones.

Jazz

The cornet was especially popular in the early jazz bands that sprang up in the US in the first half of the twentieth century. They're still used in many traditional jazz bands, though the trumpet has long had the upper hand as a modern jazz instrument. A jazz quintet often consists of a rhythm section (pianist, bassist and drummer) with a trumpet or trombone and a saxophonist. Most big bands – the biggest kind of jazz groups – have around four trumpeters, four trombonists and several saxophonists as well as a rhythm section.

Horn sections

Trumpets and trombonists also appear in a standard 'horn section', along with one or two saxes. Horn sections feature in all kinds of bands, from pop and rock to soul, salsa and funk, spicing up the music with colourful accents and sizzling riffs.

MAINLY BRASS

Brass instruments are central to concert bands and brass bands, but also to many other types of groups.

Concert bands

With some forty to one hundred musicians, the military or concert band is the biggest type of orchestra in which brass instruments play the leading role. Concert bands play many different types of music, and as well as trumpets, trombones and cornets the line-up usually includes horns, euphoniums and tubas, woodwind instruments (flutes, oboes, clarinets and saxes) and a large percussion section.

Brass bands

Brass bands contain only brass instruments and a percussion section, usually around 25 players in all. Cornets play the lead role – usually short (British) cornets, as the brass band is largely a British tradition. The standard line-up also includes E flat 'soprano' cornets, E flat horns, B flat baritones, euphoniums, trombones, tubas, one flugelhorn, and between one and five percussionists.

Show bands

Show bands do not have a specific line-up, but generally they're like smaller versions of a concert band. These groups usually perform whilst marching, though you may sometimes see them on stage or on a sports pitch. They're often accompanied by majorettes.

Uniform

Concert bands, military bands, show bands and similar groups usually perform in uniform or costume. In Britain, some bands even have a 'uniform' for the instruments – a *silver band* is a brass band in which all the musicians play a silver-plated instrument.

Other bands

There are many other types of groups in which brass instruments take centre stage, some of which only exist in certain countries or regions. Fanfare orchestras, for example, which are found in certain European countries, are similar to brass bands but usually include saxophones, whilst trumpet bands and hunting horn bands use natural instruments (those without valves or with only one).

GLOSSARY AND INDEX

This glossary contains short definitions of all the brass-related terms used in this book. There are also some words you won't find on the previous pages, but which you might come across in magazines, catalogues and books. The numbers refer to the pages where you can read more about each entry.

Amado water key See: *Water key.*

American cornet *(11–12)* The American cornet is longer than the British or European cornet.

Bach trumpet See: *Piccolo trumpet.*

Backbore *(69–70)* The inside of the *shank* of a mouthpiece. See also: *Mouthpiece.*

Background brass *(103–105)* A term used to describe brass instruments that are mostly used to accompany the melody instruments, such as the euphonium, mellophone, baritone and alto horn.

Bass trombone *(14, 50)* Type of trombone which usually has the same dimensions as a tenor trombone, but with an extra-large bore and bell. It often has two valves.

Bell *(8–9, 14, 32–33, 35–37)* The section of the instrument with the flared end. The material used for the bell and its size are important to the overall sound. Some instruments have a tuneable bell.

Bell stay *(13–14, 77)* The brace in the bell section of a trombone.

B flat instrument *(16–18)* Most trumpets, cornets

and flugelhorns are B flat instruments. If you read and play a 'C' on any of these instruments, the note that comes out is the same pitch as a B flat on a piano. All these instruments also come in many other keys (see page 101).

Booster *(70–71)* A metal cap which adds weight to a mouthpiece.

Bore *(11, 33–35, 69–70)* Bore refers to the size or shape of the inside of a tube. A wide tube has a large bore, and a narrow tube has a small bore. A straight tube has a *cylindrical bore*, and a tube that gets steadily wider has a *conical bore*. A trombone is largely cylindrical, whilst a flugelhorn is largely conical.

Bottom spring, bottom-sprung See: *Top spring, top-sprung.*

Bow *(6, 8, 14)* A bend in the tube of a brass instrument.

Brace *(9, 14, 40)* On a trumpet, cornet and flugel-horn there are various supporting 'braces' between the leadpipe and the bell. Trombones also have braces. See also: *Slide.*

Brass *(31–32)* An alloy made of lots of copper and some zinc is the material most commonly used to make brass instruments. Yellow brass contains less copper, whilst redder brass (known *rose brass*, *gold brass* or *red brass*) contains more.

British cornet See: *American cornet.*

Bugle *(100)* A 'natural' flugelhorn – one without valves.

Cases and covers *(83–84)* No brass instrument should be without some kind of case.

Conical See: *Bore.*

Convertible trombone *(50)* A trombone with a detachable F-attachment. See also: *F-attachment.*

Cornet à pistons An old name (sometimes shortened to 'piston') for the short, British cornet.

Crook See: *Tuning slide.*

C sharp slide See: *Valve slides.*

C trumpet *(17)* A 'trumpet in C', which is slightly smaller than the regular B flat trumpet. See also: *B flat instrument.*

Cup *(61–62, 65–67)* The cup-shaped part of a mouthpiece, within which your lips vibrate. See also: *Mouthpiece.*

Cylinder, cylinder valve See: *Valve.*

Cylindrical bore See: *Bore.*

D slide See: *Valve slides.*

Dual bore *(34–35)* On a dual-bore trombone, the upper slide tube has a smaller bore than the lower one. A trombone with the same bore over the entire length of its slide has a *straight bore*. Some trumpets also have a dual bore.

E flat instrument See: *B flat instrument.*

Embouchure *(20)* Your embouchure or 'lip' is your lips and jaws, and all the muscles around them, and the way you use them to play.

F-attachment *(49–52)* A tube and valve system for trombones which allows the player to lower the pitch by a fourth.

Fluegelhorn Alternative spelling for flugelhorn.

F slide See: *Valve slides.*

Gig bag *(83–84)* A padded bag for carrying instruments.

Gilded *(28)* Gold-plated. See also: *Silver plating.*

Gooseneck *(48–49)* The first piece of tubing of a trombone's bell section.

Harmonic, harmonic series *(4, 53, 98, 107)* On a brass instrument you can play a series of notes with each combination of valves pressed down (or in each slide position on a trombone). These notes are called *harmonics*, and each series of notes is a *harmonic series*. *Natural instruments* have no valves so can play the notes of one harmonic series.

Inner slide, outer slide See: *Slide.*

Insurance *(86)*

Intonation *(52–53, 81)* The better the intonation of an instrument, the easier it is to play it in tune.

Lacquer *(31–32, 56)* Most modern brass instruments are lacquered. Others are plated with silver, gold or nickel.

Leadpipe *(7–8, 11, 37–38)* The leadpipe or *mouthpipe* is the piece of tubing right after the mouthpiece receiver.

Lip See: *Embouchure.*

Low brass *(103–105)* A term used to describe low-pitched brass instruments such as baritones and tubas.

Lyre *(10)* A lyre-shaped metal clamp that attaches to a brass instrument and holds sheet music. Lyres are mostly used during marching.

affects your technique and how comfortably you can play. Factors which affect how a mouthpiece sounds and feels are weight, the size and depth of the *cup*, the width and shape of the *rim*, the size of the smallest opening (the *bore* or *throat*), and the shape and size of the *backbore* (the inside of the *shank*, the part that fits into the mouthpiece receiver of the instrument).

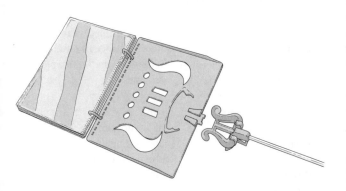

A lyre with a click-on music holding system

Microphones *(85–86)* Brass players can use either standard vocal microphones or special clip-on ones.

Monel *(45)* A copper-nickel alloy, often used for valves.

Mouthpiece *(6–8, 54, 56, 60–72, 77, 81, 94, 96)* The removable section of a brass instrument that you blow into, which greatly

Mouthpiece receiver See: *Receiver.*

Mouthpipe See: *Leadpipe.*

Mute *(24–25, 73–76)* Most mutes fit into the bell of an instrument. Practice mutes really do mute the sound, whilst others are used primarily for creating specific tone colours and sound effects.

Natural instruments *(107, 117)* Instruments without valves or a slide, which can only play harmonics. They're also known as 'signal instruments'. See also: *Harmonic.*

Nickel silver *(47)* An alloy of copper, zinc, nickel and some other metals – but no silver. Also known as *German silver, white bronze* and *alpaca.*

Outer slide, inner slide See: *Slide.*

Pedal note, pedal The lowest notes playable on a brass instrument. They are the fundamental notes of the harmonic series.

Périnet valve See: *Valve.*

Piccolo trumpet *(101)* A small, very high-sounding trumpet with four valves. Also called the 'Bach trumpet'.

Piston guides *(45, 90)* Small protrusions which make it easier to replace pistons in their valve casings in the right position.

Pocket trumpet *(102)* A very tightly 'rolled up' trumpet, which sounds the same pitch as a regular trumpet.

Practice mute *(24–25)* A type of mute which greatly reduces the volume of an instrument.

Receiver *(8)* The tube that the mouthpiece fits into. It's also called the *Venturi tube* and the *mouthpiece receiver.*

Rim *(67–68)* The section of a mouthpiece that the lips rest against. The term also refers to the edge of the bell. See also: *Mouthpiece.*

Rotary instrument *(46–47)* An instrument with rotary valves. See: *Valve.*

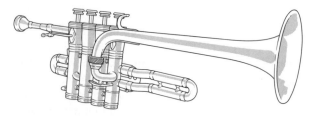

A piccolo trumpet

Piston, piston valve See: *Cornet à pistons* and *Valve.*

Rotary valve, rotor See: *Valve.*

Second-hand buying tips *(29–30, 56–59)*

Shank *(61)* The section of a mouthpiece that fits into the instrument. See also: *Mouthpiece.*

Shepherd's crook *(12)* The double bend after the valves on the short, British cornet, which has the shape of a shepherd's crook.

Signal instruments See: *Natural instruments.*

Silver plating *(31, 56)* Instead of being lacquered, an instrument may be silver-plated or even gold-plated. These precious metals last longer than lacquer. Virtually all mouthpieces are silver-plated, but gold-plated ones are also available *(71)*.

Slide *(4–5, 13–14, 34, 47, 58, 77–79, 93–94)* The slide of a trombone consists of a moveable *outer slide* and a static *inner slide* (two tubes, which have very slight bulges called *stockings* at the end). You hold the inner slide with the *inner slide brace* and move the outer slide with the *outer brace* or *slide stay.*

Slide lock *(14, 59)* A little locking mechanism at the top of the outer slide, to stop it moving of its own accord.

Slide trumpet *(99)* A very early, pre-valve trumpet, and an incorrect name for the trombone.

Soprano brass A term used to describe the higher-pitched brass instruments, such as trumpets, cornets and flugelhorns. The tenor trombone is sometimes said to be a soprano instrument, and sometimes a *low brass* instrument. See also: *Low brass.*

Stockings *(97)* Thicker sections at the ends of a trombone's inner slide tubes. See also: *Slide.*

Straight bore See: *Dual bore.*

Straight trombone *(50)* Trombone without an F-attachment.

Tenor trombone *(12–14)* The 'standard' trombone, with or without an F-attachment. See also: *F-attachment.*

Throat *(60)* The thinnest point of the tube inside a mouthpiece. See also: *Mouthpiece.*

Top spring, top-sprung

(45) On most valves, the spring is above the piston (a *top spring*). On a *bottom-sprung* valve it is underneath (a *bottom spring*).

Trigger *(11, 43–44)* A mechanism to operate the valve slide(s) on a flugelhorn. Sometimes found on trumpets and cornets too.

Tuning *(79–82)* See: *Tuning slide.*

Tuning bell, tuneable bell See: *Bell.*

Tuning crook See: *Tuning slide.*

Tuning slide *(7–8, 12, 14, 38–39, 79)* You tune a flugelhorn with the *tuning slide*, the straight section of tubing which the mouthpiece fits into. Trumpets, cornets and trombones are tuned by with a U-shaped tuning slide, which is also known as the main *tuning slide* and the *tuning crook.*

Valve *(5–6, 44–47, 57–58, 78–79, 89–92, 95, 99)* Valves make an instrument longer by redirecting the air through extra sections of tube, thereby lowering the notes produced. Most trumpets, cornets and flugelhorns have *piston valves* or *Périnet valves* in which a *piston* moves up and down to redirect the air, but on rotary trumpets and trombones with F-attachments this is done by a *rotary valve* (*rotor* or *cylinder valve*) which uses a rotating movement.

Valve casing *(8, 90, 95)* Each piston is enclosed in its own *valve casing.*

Valve group, valve cluster *(9)* The part of an instrument in which the valves are housed. Also called the *machine.*

Valve slides *(7, 8, 42–44, 92, 97)* Moveable U-shaped pieces of tubing attached to

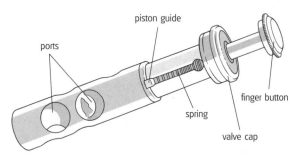

A piston valve

the valves. They are sometimes referred to just as *slides*, or named after a note which they produce, such as the *D-slide*.

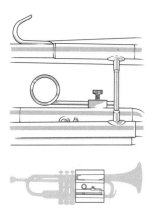

An adjustable finger ring on the third valve slide

Valve trombone *(52)* A trombone with piston valves, like a trumpet, instead of a slide.

Venturi tube See: *Receiver.*

Water *(79)* Some trombonists spray the inside of their slide with a little water before they play, to make it operate more smoothly.

Water key *(7, 9, 39–40, 58, 82)* A *water key* is a device on a brass instrument used to remove the moisture that collects in the instrument. Amado water keys are slightly smaller than the 'standard' design.

Wrap *(49–50)* A trombone with one or two valves may have an *open wrap*, in which case the extra tubing sticks out behind the instrument, or a *closed* or *traditional wrap*, in which case it lies within the bell section. See also: *F-attachment.*

WANT TO KNOW MORE?

This book gives you all the basics you need for buying, maintaining and using a trumpet, trombone, flugelhorn or cornet. If you want to know more, try consulting the magazines, books and Web sites listed below.

MAGAZINES

- *Band & Orchestra Product News* is an American magazine containing lots of information about new instruments and accessories. www.bandandorchestra.com
- *The Swiss Brass Bulletin* is also published in English. www.brass-bulletin.ch
- *ITG Journal* is the magazine of the American-based International Trumpet Guild. www.trumpetguild.org
- *The British Bandsman* is a British magazine focusing exclusively on brass bands. www.britishbandsman.com
- *Windplayer* is another American publication. www.windplayer.com
- *The Trombonist* is the journal of The British Trombone Society, PO Box 817, London SE21 7BY
- *ITA Journal* is the quarterly magazine of the International Trombone Association, Box 305338, Denton, TX 76203, USA; Fax: +1 (940) 891 3435

BOOKS

Some of the many books on brass instruments are:
- *The Cambridge Companion to Brass Instruments*, edited by Trevor Herbert and John Wallace (Cambridge University Press, Cambridge, 1997, 341 pages; ISBN 0 521 56343 7/0 521 56522 7). A series of quite dense articles about how brass instruments work, their history

and production, about playing, studying, teaching and other subjects. With glossary.

- *Brass Instruments: Their History and Development*, Anthony Baines (Dover Publications, Inc., New York, 1993, 300 pages; ISBN 0-486-27574-4). Well-illustrated guide, covering everything from shells to sousaphones.
- *The Trombonist's Handbook: A Complete Guide to Playing and Teaching the Trombone*, Reginald H. Fink (Accura Music, Ohio, 1970/1977, 145 pages; ISBN 0 918194 01 6). A very complete volume which covers, among other topics, posture, embouchure and tone production, buyers' tips, performance and ensemble playing.

INTERNET

You'll find thousands of Internet pages covering practically every brass-related subject. Try starting with one of the following Web sites, which contain frequently asked questions sections and links to other sites. And don't forget the Web sites of the magazines listed above.

- BrassWorld International: www.brass-world.com
- Internet Bandsman's "Everything Within": www.harrogate.co.uk/harrogate-band/ibew.htm
- R. Jones Trumpet Page: www.whc.net/rjones
- Trumpet Player Online: www.v-zone.com/tpo/Trumpet.html
- The British Trombone Society: www.trombone-society.org.uk
- The International Trombone Association: www.ita-web.org
- TromboneFAQ: www.brusseau.com/TromboneFAQ

Search engines

If you're using a search engine to find information, you can try searching for the name of your instrument, such as "flugelhorn", but you may have more success searching for "brass instruments" or "brasswind instruments". And you can often find a manufacturer's site at www.[brand name].com, replacing [brand name] with the name of the brand you are looking for.

ESSENTIAL DATA

In the event of your equipment being stolen or lost, or if you decide to sell it, it's useful to have all relevant data to hand. Here are two pages for those notes. For the insurance company, for the police or just for yourself.

INSURANCE

Company:

Phone: Fax:

Agent:

Phone: Fax:

Policy number:

Premium:

INSTRUMENTS AND ACCESSORIES

Make and model:

Serial number:

Value:

Specifications:

Date of purchase:

Place of purchase:

Phone: Fax:

Make and model:

Serial number:

Value:

Specifications:

Date of purchase:

Place of purchase:

Phone: Fax:

Make and model:

Serial number:

Value:

Specifications:

Date of purchase:

Place of purchase:

Phone: Fax:

Make and model:

Serial number:

Value:

Specifications:

Date of purchase:

Place of purchase:

Phone: Fax:

ADDITIONAL NOTES

....

....

....

....

....

....

....

....

....

....

....

....

....

ADDITIONAL NOTES

....
....
....
....
....
....
....
....
....
....
....
....
....
....
....
....
....
....
....
....
....
....
....
....
....
....
....
....
....
....
....
....